STRENGTH
TO
R U N

Hope and Strength in the Race of Suffering

laura wilson

WESTBOW
PRESS®
A DIVISION OF THOMAS NELSON
& ZONDERVAN

Cover photo by Karl F Mullings
KFM Designs

Backdrop photo by Stephen Probert

Author photo by Caitlin Buchanan Photography

Scripture taken from the New King James Version®. Copyright © 1982 by Thomas Nelson. Used by permission. All rights reserved.

This book is a work of non-fiction. Unless otherwise noted, the author and the publisher make no explicit guarantees as to the accuracy of the information contained in this book and in some cases, names of people and places have been altered to protect their privacy.

WestBow Press books may be ordered through booksellers or by contacting:

WestBow Press
A Division of Thomas Nelson & Zondervan
1663 Liberty Drive
Bloomington, IN 47403
www.westbowpress.com
1 (866) 928-1240

ISBN: 978-1-5127-8939-3 (sc)
ISBN: 978-1-5127-8940-9 (hc)
ISBN: 978-1-5127-8938-6 (e)

Library of Congress Control Number: 2017909040

Print information available on the last page.

WestBow Press rev. date: 06/23/2017

Therefore we also, since we are surrounded by so great a cloud of witnesses, let us lay aside every weight, and the sin which so easily ensnares us, and let us run with endurance the race that is set before us, looking unto Jesus, the author and finisher of our faith, who for the joy that was set before Him endured the cross, despising the shame, and has sat down at the right hand of the throne of God.

Hebrews 12:1–2

In this race of faith, I want to run well.

Thank you again to all of our precious family members and friends for praying us through this. We truly couldn't have run this race without your love, encouragement, support, and prayers! We continue to be in awe of how faithful you have been in running alongside us—from the starting blocks all the way through the finish line!

I am dedicating this story to my family and friends who loved and supported me so completely and tenderly during every step of this grueling race. This story is equally dedicated to all of the brave souls who have run a similar race or are in the middle of their race now. I pray that you, too, can hold tight to His promises and allow Him to be your STRENGTH TO RUN.

But those who hope in the Lord will renew their strength.
They will soar on wings like eagles; they will run and not grow weary,
they will walk and not be faint.
Isaiah 40:31 (New International Version)

CONTENTS

FOREWORD

As I sit here and think about what I should say that would best describe this epic battle, this trying race, and this incredible woman, all I keep coming back to is my wife's repetitive words: "By God's amazing grace." By His grace, we were put in the battle together. By His grace, we were given four beautiful children who needed their mother. By His grace, He placed the right people in our lives at just the right time. By His grace, we rose up to stand strong in the onslaught of the enemy, and by His grace, He gently carried us when things went outside of our plans. Also by His grace, we will continue to enjoy another day with those we love and treasure, fully knowing that we are not in control of our destiny, but we know the One who is.

I feel so blessed to have been given the opportunity to grow alongside my wife as she fiercely faced the new enemy in our lives, yet somehow stayed tender and gentle, during the heat of the battle, toward our Savior, our family and friends, and toward the healthcare workers and total strangers who were suddenly in her life. She could barely lift herself off the bed or out of a chair at times in order to get on the road to the Mayo Clinic, but she would reach out and encourage so many as she made her way there and back. She was a light that could not be hidden; not by her own will, but by the knowledge that she was in God's capable and loving hands. I would often walk behind her just to watch as her light filled the room; a room full of very sick, sad, and angry patients who somehow saw in her a spirit of confidence, combined with humility, that gave them the hope they were so desperately seeking.

As I was allowed to read this book for the first time, the memories flooded back with each chapter, and I once again realized just how big this race was and how insignificant I felt. There was nothing I could do but watch a giant oncoming Mack truck bear down on my wife and hit her at full speed as I helplessly stood by, waiting and praying for her to survive the impact. Cancer is a killer of hope and dreams, and it has the ability to strip us of everything we love. But God had a different plan for this race, one that saw Laura make a long, come-from-behind sprint to the finish line. This was a race that often was just as hard emotionally and mentally on us as her family as it was for her physically. Cancer has no feelings, and yet somehow the feelings of every emotion possible, and the love of our family and friends, coupled with a merciful Savior, is what showed us all *amazing grace.*

Mark Wilson

As you read, you will find un-edited journal entries directly from our CaringBridge website to help tell this story. Prior to my diagnosis, I didn't even know CaringBridge existed. My good friends Anita and Flower made a site for us that provided a way to communicate the details of our journey with others. Flower's brother had gone through a difficult battle with cancer, and both he and the family found CaringBridge to be very helpful. It turned out to be a wonderful blessing in the midst of an extremely challenging time for us as well. It served as a communication vehicle, and I believe it was a helpful tool for us to write down the details. It also allowed those close to us an effective way to coordinate help. The CaringBridge gave our prayer warriors specific needs to pray for as we posted our many detailed updates, and we were able to connect with family and friends all over the country and the world who cared about us. We truly felt the prayers of our faithful friends holding us up each day. The sweet, encouraging messages I received daily were an added treasure to me. Reading the posts was like opening the mailbox every day and finding a handful of special cards just for me.

INTRODUCTION

It was a beautiful June morning, the sun hidden by a slight cloud cover to make it a pleasant eighty degrees in our mountain town. Flagstaff is known for its close proximity to the Grand Canyon, the red rocks of Sedona, and the San Francisco Peaks; it's a tourist town of about seventy-five thousand where people come to enjoy the clean air and the dark night sky. One can rarely make a quick stop at the grocery store without running into a familiar face. Although Flagstaff has grown leaps and bounds since our family moved here in 1977, it still has a small-town feel. It is the town I love and the town that I call home.

The night before the race, I didn't sleep much at all, yet I knew I desperately needed sleep if I was going to make it. I tried to imagine the day ahead and wondered how it would go and how many people would be there. I doubted I would feel good enough to go, and thought Mark and the kids might have to go without me. I silently wondered if I should just stay home with our precious kids and let the race go on without me. That way I could avoid all of the dreaded comments and questions from others.

Race day came. The kids put on their new purple t-shirts, grabbed their water bottles and sunscreen, and we headed for the car. The fifteen-minute drive from our house was quiet. The kids were still not sure why they were awake so early on what should have been a lazy Saturday morning. Mark and I didn't talk much. We had no idea what to expect when we drove into the bumpy, dirt parking lot of Buffalo Park that morning. We had been there many times before, walking hand-in-hand, pushing a fussy baby in a stroller, or cheering on one of our kids as they ran their heart out in the city-wide elementary school cross-country meet.

Today was entirely different. I was overwhelmed. I knew we couldn't make it through this medical emergency financially, but I wasn't sure how I felt about a fundraiser in my honor. Mark was my designated spokesperson, and he did a great job of thanking everyone and speaking on my behalf. I stood alongside him in my sunglasses as if to hide my ever-changing, now very sickly outward appearance.

Looking back on that day still overwhelms me. I am in awe of the support shown to us by this community. Hundreds of people were running to support our family: people from church, from work, from the Fire Department. Doctors, nurses, moms with strollers and backpacks, old friends, new friends, and almost all of our family—they were all there for me. Their participation in the Run with Laura sent a strong message that they would not abandon our family during this grueling race.

I still see a purple shirt in town every once in a while, and it takes my breath away. I have a very special friend who sends me selfies or a sweet text message every time she puts it on. Mine is folded carefully and kept in a special storage box, but one of the medals that were given out to participants that day hangs from my dresser mirror.

I *hate* to run. I don't just dislike it; I really do hate it. Running is extremely hard, and I think it is boring. It can be intimidating, and it takes a lot of practice and dedication. Although I am fully aware that there is a multitude of health benefits like decreased heart disease and type 2 diabetes, improved blood pressure, increased lung function, and stronger muscles, I just don't like it.

I have a lot of friends who run, and they have tried to convince me that there is some magical moment when running becomes enjoyable. Many people say you just have to be mentally tough, and you need to "power through." Well, I have never gotten there. I still hate it. Ironically, I ran track in high school, but even then I didn't necessarily enjoy running. I remember asking my coach why the sprinters had to run long distance in practice. He tried to explain the benefits of distance training and conditioning, but it just didn't make sense in my stubborn, teenage mind.

In my day, we had a 50-yard dash, and I loved it (after all, it was 1985). I think the only place you can still find a 50-yard dash is at an elementary school field day where children are awarded generic participation ribbons for their valiant running efforts. At the time, I felt like I could run fairly fast for a short distance on the all-weather, rubberized track. I also ran the 100, the 200, and the 4 x 100 relay. Each one of these events is essentially an all-out sprint from the startling sound of the gun to the finish line. Perfecting the start was a challenge, for sure, and trying to stay somewhat relaxed while trying to run at top speed was something I don't think I ever mastered. The 4 x 100 is where four athletes each run approximately 100 meters, or a quarter of the track. This event not only requires speed from each of the runners but precision in the transfer of the aluminum baton. The baton has to be exchanged within a specific marked area on the track, and your team faces disqualification if this is not done correctly. The runner in front simply extends her arm backward in the hopes that the quickly approaching runner behind her will accurately place it in her hand as she begins to accelerate. I'm getting stressed just thinking about it. I wasn't all that great at running then, and I am definitely not great at it now.

As an adult, I don't run very often or very far, and when I do, I am usually complaining the entire time. I often find myself counting my every footstep and bargaining with myself about how far I will go before I can take a break. Hey, running isn't for everyone, right? I do enjoy walking and hiking, and I will occasionally throw in some short bursts of running here and there to keep my heart rate up, usually where it is flat or downhill. That is about the extent of my running history.

It is almost funny that I have titled this book *Strength to Run,* because I hate it that much.

Clearly I was called in February of 2013, as Hebrews 12:1 says, to "run with endurance the race" God had set before me. I didn't sign up for this race, and I had no idea what it would be like. I had no practice or training to prepare me. This was a race that would require much of me and my family, and without God-given, steady determination and perseverance, I knew we would not be able to run it alone or in our own strength.

What I did know is that my sovereign God ordered and ordained each of my steps before I was even born. He knew before the beginning of time that this race was on the horizon. He even impressed upon me to take pictures of my feet all throughout this race, long before I knew

I would write a book and long before I knew the title and theme of the story I was to write. My God has custom-designed each of my days for me, even the dark, ugly ones. In His perfect sovereignty, He allowed this difficult period of pain and suffering in my life, and by His strength and grace, He has used and continues to use my story to proclaim His glory and to show me how to walk (or run!) by faith.

So take seriously the story that God has given you to live.
It's time to read your own life, because your story
is the one that could set us all ablaze.
Dan Allender, *To Be Told*

CHAPTER 1

Foundations

Life seldom turns out exactly the way we expected it to be.

Life can bring hardships that really hurt. It brings us a lot of joyous moments, and it can also bring gut-wrenching pain. We might experience the joys of a new job, watching a red sunset on the edge of the Grand Canyon, or sleeping under the stars. We could be surprised by developing an unlikely friendship, or maybe we enjoy a great meal, stay at a quirky bed-and-breakfast, or explore a new mountain trail. It might be the thrill of riding the rides at Disneyland until midnight, marveling at a newborn baby as you hold it in your arms for the first time, watching snowflakes fall on a cozy Christmas morning, or just enjoying a great cup of coffee with a friend. The list is different for everyone.

We also experience unexpected and unwelcomed adversity in our lives to some degree. Right now, you might be suffering from ongoing illness, loneliness, deep depression, debilitating anxiety and fear, a destructive addiction, or chronic pain. You may have endured a painful childhood, lost your job, or experienced the loss of someone precious to you. You might be in an exhausting and difficult relationship, or you may be experiencing financial strain, suffering through the pain of betrayal by someone who was supposed to love and protect you, or experiencing the heartache of a rebellious child.

Unfortunately, we live in a fallen world that often brings pain, suffering, and heartache. We aren't usually planning on it, but it comes. We might be asking why a loving God allows these brutally difficult things to happen, and it can be really hard to see God's purposes in our present grief. Most of the time, we can't see a purpose at all. And the truth is that we might not see a purpose in this lifetime. Sometimes all we can see is the rocky terrain. The black clouds building, and the darkness looming ahead. The pain. The distance. The cliffs. The hurdles and the rugged, dangerous mountain trails. Still somehow, even when we can't see where we are going and when our strength is gone, we are called to trust Him. We are to trust Him when the race seems lost and the end is nowhere in sight.

In these dark, exhausting places is where He often meets us with abounding love, mercy, grace, and strength.

The pages of this book share with you a story of hope. Hope in a God who held me close when my life was upside down. Hope in a God who walked with me when I could no longer be the mom I love to be and when the life of my family was in complete chaos. And hope in a God who cared in the midst of suffering and who picked me up when I could no longer stand.

I am sitting down in front of my computer to write for the very first time. I have to confess that I don't really know how to write a book, or even where to start, but I do know that God has called me to write this story down. There was no pretending that I didn't hear or that I didn't understand. He made it undeniably clear. I am certain that, just as with everything else in my life, if it is something He wants me to do, He will give me the determination and strength, the time, the energy, and the ability to do it. I am trusting Him for each and every word.

This is a story of learning to persevere with faith and trust in a sovereign God who holds every part of my life in His loving, powerful hands. This book was written by someone who has experienced the mess of cancer and the ravages of its brutal treatment yet miraculously emerged as an overcomer on the other side. At the same time, and with a heavy heart, I am reminded that not all cancer stories have good endings. Cancer doesn't seem to have any boundaries, and it doesn't follow the rules. I have a high school friend who was diagnosed with cancer just a few short months before I was, and her story is entirely different—her time on earth has recently come to an end. Six members in our small church have lost the battle with cancer within the last two years. Another young mom is sadly losing her battle as I write this. Sometimes these harsh realities feel almost too raw to process. I grapple with why God, in His sovereignty, has chosen to heal and restore me and has not healed others. I struggle with a weird sense of guilt, and I wrestle with this every day. Yet this is a place in my life where I have to completely trust in His plan. I don't understand how or why He writes the stories He does, but I have to trust that He knows what He is doing.

God gives each of us a story to tell—this just happens to be mine.

I was born in Arcadia, California, on February 29, 1968, to a mother I never knew. I was a big baby, weighing nine pounds and three ounces at birth, and I was twenty-two inches long. My birth mother carried me for ten long months, held my warm, wet little body in her arms, and took me home where she was already raising three children (ages six, seven, and eight) on her own. She cared for me for several weeks before she handed me over to a complete stranger at the Los Angeles County Bureau of Adoption. I do not know the details behind this difficult decision, and I do not know the specific involvement of my birth father; all I know is that it must have been a terribly painful time in her life. I cannot know the agony and heartache of walking out of those adoption agency doors that April day in Southern California. It is something I imagine only women who have walked a similar road can understand. My birth mother gave me life and, out of deep, sacrificial love, made the difficult choice of adoption for me. As a mother of four myself, I can't even begin to imagine the deep wounds leading up to her decision. I am still in awe of her bravery, courage, and selflessness—and I am forever grateful that she loved me that much. In this emotionally painful time, she chose life over death because she knew somehow in the depth of her soul that my life was valuable. I am guessing that abortion would probably have been easier at the time. It was common in the late sixties but did not reach its peak until 1973 when the Supreme Court legalized the procedure in the landmark Roe vs. Wade case. The pro-abortion agencies have worked diligently ever since to make it sound "easy" and morally "acceptable." I read recently that there is only one adoption for every 149 abortions.

That is a staggering statistic. My birth mother made a selfless decision against overwhelming odds. Somehow she was able to put herself aside and consider my well-being above her own. Aborting me would have been final, but adoption was a new beginning.

Because of God's unfathomable love for me and by His abounding grace, I have somehow never questioned who I am or wrestled with why I was given up for adoption. A lot of people really struggle with this. I just haven't. My mom reminded me of a time on a long drive home when I asked her why I was given away. She gave a tender answer, and I gazed out the window in utter silence. My parents suspected I would be asking more questions and would possibly want to find my biological parents. To their surprise, I never really brought it up again.

In His perfect sovereignty, God orchestrated the details for the Los Angeles adoption agency to place me into the loving arms of Alan and Virginia Strnad. After spending about a month with a foster family, my parents brought me home to a very excited big brother and a room decorated with pink and white gingham on May 16, 1968. This is where life really began.

I was a happy baby girl with blue eyes, blonde hair, and dimples. My eyes (which are now two different colors) were both bluish-gray as an infant, as are most fair-skinned blonde babies. My right eye slowly changed to a hazel color over the course of my first year. My only brother, Paul, had been adopted through the same adoption agency but from a different birth mother in 1965. He was almost three when my parents brought me home. Our standard American family of four lived on a palm tree–lined street in West Covina. We lived in a single-story ranch-style house, and my dad worked as a civil engineer for the State of California. He worked on the California Aqueduct, along with other projects. In 1970, we moved to Alaska so that my dad could design runways in small towns and villages and later work on part of the Anchorage airport. I am sure it was a sad day for my mom's parents, who lived nearby in California, to say goodbye, knowing we would be so far away.

Moving from California to Alaska was a big adjustment for our family of four, although I was a baby so I didn't have much of an opinion at the time. We had spent our long, sunny days in beautiful Southern California, playing with neighborhood friends, eating plums right off the tree in our backyard, and walking to the 7-Eleven down the street for a Slurpee. Before we knew it, we were off to the tiny halibut fishing village of Homer, Alaska—population back then probably all of two thousand.

Driving the long, dirt Alaska Highway to Homer allowed for many deep conversations between my mom and dad while Paul and I tried to entertain ourselves in the big back seat. There were no DVD players, no Gameboys, and no iPads. We simply looked out the window, played games, slept, looked at books, and probably asked, "Are we there yet?" at least a hundred times.

My mom remembers a conversation she had with my dad during that long drive. She was concerned that she didn't know enough about the Bible to teach us about God, and she wanted to be able to teach us the "right things" as we grew up. The topic didn't come up much more after that, and life went along. Our family spent two years in Homer, then moved to Anchorage, then to King Salmon, and finally to Glen Allen while my dad was involved in various engineering projects. The only available house to rent in Homer happened to be directly across the street from a church where a Fall Revival was going on. There were nightly meetings and music. The pastor and his wife kindly invited my parents to come, and that night my mom and dad heard for the first time about a Savior who gave his life on a cross for their sins. They attended a few more church meetings out of curiosity and heard the pastor urge those in the audience to "give their all for the Lord." My dad initially thought this meant they wanted all of his money, but soon understood that the Lord wanted his heart and not his checkbook.

One summer evening, he went across the street to talk to the pastor and to ask a few more questions. The pastor offered his daughter's babysitting services so that my mom could come and visit, too. The gospel message was perfectly clear that night. My mom and dad both gave their hearts to the Lord that night at the Sekins' small kitchen table in Homer on October 8, 1970. God's plan had been at work all along, and He was busy orchestrating the details in His perfect timing. He was ordering my parents' steps without them even knowing what was happening. Their hearts were instantly transformed, and my dad felt an almost immediate calling to ministry. My parents' faithful walk with God would be a lifetime example for me.

We were in Alaska for less than five years. I have a few blurry memories, but not many because of my young age. I remember snowmobiles, my blue Bambi sheets, a few special toys, lots of snow, and my tiny bedroom. At one point, we lived in a small, ten-foot-wide mobile home where Paul and I could both remove the drawers that were built into the wall between our rooms and crawl through. There were nights we played for hours when we were supposed to be sleeping. My mom was gracious to let Paul and me keep a large yellow expandable Winnie the Pooh tunnel up in the small hallway of our trailer. We would all crawl down the long, narrow hall to the bathroom, even my mom and dad! I attended kindergarten in Glen Allen, and Paul was in the third grade. My mom likes to tell the story of my kindergarten teacher asking her one day if she knew I could read and asking permission to test me. I was reading fifth grade level books. She wanted me to skip a couple of grades at the time, but my mom felt that I was thriving with my sweet little kindergarten friends, so I stayed put. She is always proud to say I taught myself to read and that it all started with Sesame Street. Thank you, Bert and Ernie! My kindergarten teacher also liked to put me in charge of the class when she had to leave the room on occasion. I wish I could remember that more vividly. I must have thought I was really something.

The four of us enjoyed Alaska, and it remains my mom and dad's favorite place on earth. They would love to live in a little cabin overlooking the Kenai Peninsula, eat moose burgers, and wear mukluks all year long if they could. I do remember the big snowy mountains. And I remember our brown house in Anchorage the most. I must have been four or five at the time. I remember special dolls and stuffed animals that I treasured and our piano in the living room that left me with a scar on my forehead when I ran into it one day. We had good friends across the street and next door that we played with during the long summer days. In the winter, we built tunnels through the snow down the sidewalks and watched moose walk right over our fence and through our backyard. My dad even built us our very own ice rink! With the daylight hours ranging from five hours in January to nineteen hours in July, a regular bedtime was a constant challenge for my mom.

Before they knew what hit them, my parents' lives and their plans were changing. My dad spent his last year in Alaska as a full-time student at Alaska Bible College (1973–74) and was no longer interested in his engineering career (much to the chagrin of his parents, especially Grandma Strnad). First exposed to rescue mission ministry at the Anchorage Rescue Mission with their local church, God was preparing the hearts of my parents for what was to come.

Our family moved to Portland, Oregon in 1974 so that my dad could attend Bible school for the next three years. My mom held down the fort and worked as a medical records decoder at a hospital while putting my dad through school. My dad began volunteering at the Portland Rescue Mission, and he and my mom quickly fell in love with ministering to broken, hurting, homeless people.

Paul and I loved being kids. I remember both of us crying when we had to say goodbye to our neighborhood friends, get in the car, and head for Arizona in 1977. We didn't think we would ever be able to make new friends. So began God's sovereign hand in bringing us to the small mountain town of Flagstaff, where my parents would run a rescue mission for more than thirty-one years.

Before arriving in Flagstaff, our 1964 red Mercury that my parents had purchased right off the line made its way from Oregon all the way to the Wi-Wi-Ta Resort on Woman Lake in Minnesota for a big family reunion late that summer. Grandma and Grandpa Strnad and each of my dad's siblings and their families stayed in their own cabin and got together throughout the day for swimming, fishing, boating, waterskiing, and canoeing. Some of my favorite childhood memories involved staying up after midnight playing Hearts with Grandma and playing pool in the resort lodge. I think we were allowed to stay up much later during our week in Minnesota because we couldn't really go anywhere or get into much trouble. After all, we were on vacation. We listened to music and played foosball for hours. I was able to slip my thin hand and wrist into the slot on the side where the balls came out and push the wooden piece where the balls rested. Needless to say, we played a lot of games on one quarter! We thought we were pretty big stuff as we listened to new songs by Stevie Nicks, Rod Stewart, Tom Petty, and the Bee Gees from the old juke box in the corner as it flipped 45 vinyl records.

We enjoyed playing practical jokes on the lodge staff and on Grandma by placing a plastic pile of dog poop or spilled milk in various places and hiding to watch people's reactions. The hot, summer days went by slowly, and we didn't want them to ever come to an end. I learned how to bait a hook with a live worm with Grandpa Strnad on the old wooden dock. I unintentionally killed a lot of fish that day as I tried to figure out how to remove a hook from the fishes' mouths. I remember a time on a later Minnesota trip when Grandpa caught a baby duck by mistake, and he was distraught about it (so was the mama duck). The duck had been playing with the bobber when it spotted a wiggly worm beneath the water's surface. Before we could get the line out of the water, the duck dove down and was hooked. I watched Grandpa slowly pull the baby duck in and work diligently to free him.

During that long, hot week at the lake, it was always a special treat to go "into town," and there was one day that we looked forward to the most. We all piled into our rented aluminum boats, powered by a small outboard motor, and drove through the bay into town. It only took about thirty minutes. Grandpa bought ice cream for all of us and took us into the tackle store to buy more bobbers and worms. We always liked looking at the giant Northern pike and long-nose gar mounted on the wooden store walls. But we weren't really there to look at dead fish mounted on an old store wall. We were there for the turtle races that were held every Wednesday afternoon in the small town of Longville where we "rented" a turtle for a dollar. After paying, we would receive a turtle race button to pin on our shirts, and a numbered sticker. The turtle with a matching number was then placed in a hot, paved circle in the middle of Main Street (poor turtle!). The first turtle to get to the outside of the circle won a prize. I don't remember exactly what the prize was, but I know I always wanted my turtle to get to the championship round. When the race was over, we returned our hot, exhausted turtles and enjoyed a fried chicken lunch at a local café with Grandma and Grandpa.

When the week was over, our family of four and our fluffy white poodle mix, Heidi, made the long, hot, 1,700-mile trip to Flagstaff, Arizona. We made a few traditional stops along the way at places like Dodge City, Kansas, Four Corners, and the famous corner in Winslow, Arizona from the Eagles song. Our big red car pulled into Flagstaff on historic Route 66, and we were greeted by the beautiful San Francisco Peaks, the highest point in all of Arizona. We made a left on San Francisco Street and pulled up in front of the Sunshine Rescue Mission on July 7, 1977.

At that time, the mission was a two-story brick building with a turquoise entrance and a big fire escape clearly visible from the street. There was a cinder rock front area with an old, wooden bench on each side of the front door, painted to match the turquoise trim around the large paned windows. We have a family picture from that day in which I was wearing brown, bell-bottomed corduroy pants (it was 1977, remember?) and a shirt that said "Foxy" in big letters. The O was a fox's head. Really, Mom? Did you let me wear that shirt in public? My mom recently reminded me that one of my grandmothers had bought that shirt for me, so I should probably thank Grandma Strnad.

The rescue mission staff was thrilled to meet us. They had been specifically praying for a new superintendent when my mom had called about job possibilities several months earlier. The staff welcomed our family warmly and knew instantly that the rescue mission would never be the same.

Although we had purchased a single-wide mobile home in a neighborhood away from the mission when we first came to Flagstaff, our family initially lived in a one-room apartment upstairs in the mission because my parents were working around the clock. When I say "apartment," what I really mean is a twelve by sixteen room with four cinder block walls that were painted a terrible yellow with two very large windows that looked down over a rowdy local bar next door. We commonly fell asleep to the beat of loud dance music, people talking, laughing, and yelling, and the routine sounds of drunken brawls in the alley below. I don't know how we survived that episode in our lives. I was only nine and Paul was twelve. We must have driven each other crazy, but we learned patience. Needless to say, it wasn't long before the four of us moved into a newly constructed apartment behind the mission where our selfless parents slept on a pullout couch so that Paul and I could have our own rooms. "Behind the mission" meant that our front door opened up to the back door of the mission where people came in and out regularly and where donations were made.

Growing up at the mission was pretty fun, actually. The men and women who stayed there became part of our everyday life, and the mission staff members often became a part of our family. We ate a lot of our family dinners at the kitchen table in the mission as my mom worked over a big commercial stove making dinner for thirty to forty homeless people. As the mission was eventually able to hire additional staff, we were finally able to move into our home in 1981, although my dad still had to spend many long nights at the mission. This is the home where my parents still live with their dog, Annie.

For more than thirty-one years, my brother and I were privileged to watch our mom and dad serve tirelessly and extend abounding love and grace to others. They gave everything they had, not only for us but for the homeless, hurting people who came through the doors of the rescue mission. They gave of their time, their energy, their money, and their possessions. But most of all, they gave their hearts. They had no barriers, no prejudices, no standards. They loved unconditionally, expecting nothing (and most often receiving nothing) in return. I can still picture my dad sitting in a snowstorm on the wooden bench outside the mission with his arm around a local drunk. I can see my mom cooking a midnight meal for a stranded woman and her three hungry, dirty, barefoot children. They gave, and they gave, and they gave. They were often taken advantage of, stolen from, and even punched in the face on occasion. Nothing seemed to deter them. I didn't realize at the time how much I would glean from watching my parents serve. This is where I began to understand grace.

Paul and I attended a small Christian school on the east side of town for the first three years in Flagstaff. For me, that was fourth, fifth, and sixth grade. Girls were not allowed to wear pants, and I never did understand that. I was known to hide jeans in my backpack on occasion and trade them out for my "gauchos" every once in a while. Why gauchos were better than jeans didn't make any sense to me either.

The Christian school was fine, but I wanted to go to a public school for seventh grade. I spent my middle and high school years in the public schools. Paul wanted to stay on at the Christian school a while longer and then spent a year or two in the same public high school.

After being teased and tormented about my different-colored eyes on the bus ride to school the first week, my dad graciously drove me to school most days on his way to work. There were times that I sat in the passenger side of an old white truck that said "Sunshine Rescue Mission" on the side in green letters. A couple years later, the mission purchased a large utility truck that had "JESUS LOVES YOU" painted on the side with a big sun and all of its rays stretching across the entire side of the truck. I don't care who you are, but that is never cool when you are in high school!

Other than my traumatizing means of transportation, junior high and high school were fun years for me. I was always a fairly independent kid, I was a good student, and I made friends quickly. I attended church and went to youth group. I found my fair share of trouble with friends and put my poor mother through a lot of sleepless nights, I am sure. I managed to do well in school, surprisingly even in chemistry and algebra, which was largely due to a smart friend who helped me understand the periodic table and to my dad for his unrelenting explanations of algebraic equations.

I graduated from Flagstaff High School in 1986 with big hair and blue high heels.

I knew I wanted to start college right away. I received grants and scholarships and began attending Northern Arizona University full time that fall, and I worked in an insurance office for the next several years. My boss was the husband of my high school Spanish teacher, Mrs. Evans, who is still a very dear friend of mine. He was very supportive of my education and allowed me the flexibility to work around my class schedule. I received a bachelor's degree in Speech/Language Pathology in 1990, thanks in part to my aunt Mary who sparked my interest in a field I wasn't even aware of. I took the introductory course after her recommendation and was hooked. I went on to receive my master's degree in 1992 and have worked as a speech/language pathologist ever since.

This career has been a perfect fit for me over the years, and I really enjoy my job. I have been able to work in all kinds of settings and make my own schedule for the most part. This has allowed me to work part time and be home most of the time with my kids. I wouldn't change that for the world! As they have gotten busier, I have been able to set my own schedule and work more while they are in school and still be done in time to pick them up from school to spend quality time with them or to attend their after school activities. I have enjoyed all kinds of work environments, from evaluating little ones in their homes on the Navajo and Hopi reservations and teaching graduate level courses in communication sciences, to providing therapy services to children and adults in their homes. I have also spent some time in preschools, hospitals, and long-term care facilities. Being bilingual has allowed me to use my Spanish to work with some beautiful families and their children. God also gave me an interest and an expertise in feeding and swallowing that would, ironically, come in handy later.

After a series of not-the-best relationship choices and some painful mistakes, I met my husband of almost twenty-three years. Mark and I actually went to the same high school, but he was two years behind me, and we did not know each other at the time. At one point, I was a scorekeeper for the wrestling team (in those days, I was actually called a "mat maid" if you can believe that), and he was a top wrestler on the team. At that time, however, he weighed only ninety-eight pounds and was about five feet tall. As we became acquainted years later, it took me a while to connect the high school Mark Wilson with the now six-foot-one, 195-pound, broad-shouldered, good-looking fireman.

I officially got to know my soul mate in a large group of mutual friends during the summer of 1993. I was playing on a women's city softball team, and he was playing on a men's team. We got to know each other in a group at first and had fun going out to eat and playing foosball after softball games. (I used to be able to beat him back in those days, but not anymore.) Mark and I did not officially start dating for a while but soon really enjoyed spending time together. We had a lot in common and both had a Christian upbringing. He was a new firefighter with an exciting job and had just bought his first house on a beautiful piece of property just two acres away from his parents. He enjoyed going out with his new fire department buddies and spent a lot of time hunting. He was fairly spontaneous and was typically late to everything. My job with Indian Children's Program had me traveling back and forth to the Navajo and Hopi reservations, and I had just bought my first little house about twenty miles south of town and was having fun fixing it up. I enjoyed the outdoors but had never hunted or killed anything. I liked organizing and planning ahead and was usually a few minutes early to everything.

After about a year of dating and surviving a painful breakup, Mark and I and were married in a beautiful aspen grove on October 8, 1994. Some of my girlfriends and bridesmaids stayed with me at Mark's house the night before the wedding so that we could all get ready together the next day. Paul was at the house a lot the day before as we worked together preparing fruit and vegetable trays and fancy hors d'oeuvres for the reception. A woman from the church Mark grew up in was coordinating the food, but we were contributing and helping as much as we could. As two o'clock got closer, I put my wedding dress on in a small hunting trailer we had parked days before on a forest road near the ceremony location. I spent a little longer than expected in the hunting trailer anxiously waiting for Mark to drive up in his red Toyota truck. I was not exaggerating when I told you he was typically late to everything—even our wedding!

I finally heard the sound of his truck and knew the ceremony could get started. I carefully stepped out of the trailer and could feel the warm mountain sun on my back. I was tenderly escorted by both my dad and my brother, and we talked and laughed as we walked over the golden aspen leaves that had blanketed the ground. We enjoyed watching my niece and nephew hold hands as they dropped flower petals along the trail and carried the rings. The train of my beautiful, beaded white dress with the huge poufy sleeves dragged through the dirt and rocks as another nephew struggled to keep it off the ground. We walked down the long aisle between rows of white wooden chairs filled with friends and family. Two longtime friends sang and played the guitar. We were married that beautiful fall day by my dad, vowing to love only each other for a lifetime...for better or for worse. Mark's dad gently read a beautiful prayer for us, and my dad performed the ceremony. Our wedding day was absolutely perfect. It was seventy degrees, the sun was shining, the quaking aspen leaves were golden and the outdoors smelled amazing. This mountain town I loved so much was a fitting backdrop for the beginning of my new life as a wife and as a maker of a home. I would come to love and appreciate its close-knit community in invaluable ways in the years to come.

After the ceremony and pictures, an entourage of vehicles drove back to Mark's parents' house for our outdoor reception. The large grassy area was immaculately trimmed, and every flower was in its place. There were white tents and round tables with white tablecloths. Handmade dried flower arrangements in wooden baskets were in the middle of each table. We enjoyed a late afternoon buffet-style dinner, cut the cake, tossed the bouquet and garter, had a quick toast of sparkling cider, and we were off on our ten-day honeymoon to British Columbia. We were so excited to leave!

After our first trip as newlyweds, Mark and I drove our brand new silver Toyota Forerunner home from the Phoenix airport to begin our lives together. We talked all the way home and were so excited to see the first glimpse of the beautiful San Francisco Peaks. They are always a welcome sight after two hours of driving in the desert. Sitting on the teal carpet of our small rock house, we opened wedding gifts for hours. I had so much fun finding places for new dishes and towels and tried desperately to turn what had been a bachelor pad into a home.

CHAPTER 2

Mom, What's This?

Mark and I were happy newlyweds for only fifteen short months before we became parents. God started our family with a perfect baby boy on January 30, 1996, and we were given just a tiny glimpse of how deeply our heavenly Father loves us. We loved little Kyle Robert with our entire being and treasured every milestone. He went everywhere with us, and he was so much fun! We read every book there was, wrestled and played for hours, explored everything with awe and wonder, hiked and camped, played with plastic animals over and over, and watched Disney movies until we had every line memorized. Life was good and we were content with our little family.

On May 7, of 1999, we fell in love with another perfect baby boy. We brought Avery Cole home to our newly built house just an acre away from the rock house. From the day we brought Avery home from the hospital, Kyle couldn't get enough of him. He was so thrilled to have a baby brother and wanted to hold him constantly. Avery's smile absolutely captivated all three of us. When he smiled, his whole body smiled along with him. He was a delight and wanted to do everything his big brother did. We now had two beautiful boys to love and enjoy. We read all of our books again and bought new ones, we wrestled and played some more, and we continued to explore and learn new things. We still hiked and camped, colored, painted, and watched Disney movies. We especially enjoyed watching the boys learn how to play together. They danced, ran, made guns out of anything and everything, dug holes, and played in the mud. A close friendship formed early on.

A third perfect baby boy was born on May 20′ of 2002, and we loved him just the same. Carter Lane charmed us with his big personality from the minute he came into the world. He was a blessed little boy with two older brothers who absolutely adored him. Kyle was now six years old and in first grade, and Avery was three. How they loved to make Carter smile and laugh! When Kyle went off to school, Avery and Carter cried. They eventually recovered and would play all day together creating Lego masterpieces, painting, reading books, and making messes. They loved going with me to pick Kyle up from school at three thirty. It was like the day started all over again once Kyle was back home where they were convinced he belonged.

Raising a bunch of boys was exciting. If there is one thing I have learned about raising boys, it is that they are *really* different from girls! They are energetic, busy, messy, fast, loud, tiring, and sometimes downright scary! We have spent a lot of time playing in the dirt, exploring the outdoors, building things, destroying things, shooting things, throwing rocks, and collecting bugs, lizards, snakes, and frogs. We have enjoyed camping, hunting, boating, and fishing. And then there is riding bikes, skates, skateboards, skis, snowboards, go-karts, and four-wheelers. We have settled many arguments, watched a lot of sports, and made countless trips to the emergency room. When we found out we were having another baby in September of 2004, it seemed that the Wilson family was going to have only boys. We were okay with that. Mothers of boys know that once you have two or three boys, adding another one is really not that big of a deal.

What a surprise we had when Danica Christine graced the world with her presence on May 28, 2005 (now *three* May birthdays!). The color pink arrived along with this beautiful baby girl that day. I honestly think every gift I received at her baby shower was pink. She was precious and sweet and brought a completely different emotion into our family. A tender, bubbly little girl has a way of changing the entire family, especially the heart of her daddy. Danica was loved by her three brothers who fought over who got to hold her next or who could help feed her. They loved showing her how to throw a ball and shoot a gun. She jumped in with both feet and played in the dirt, dug holes, threw rocks, built things, shot things, and collected little creatures right along with the boys. At the same time, she loved babies and sparkly things, she talked more than all the boys put together, she loved to sing, and she wanted everyone's undivided attention.

Over the course of ten years, we now had four children, almost perfectly spaced apart by three years. Our three energetic boys kept us on our toes, and our girl brought a necessary component of sweet to our family. We loved every minute of parenting, and I thoroughly enjoyed my time at home being a mama.

My grandmother on my mom's side, Beulah Root, had moved in with us shortly before Danica was born. We had converted our former garage into a studio apartment for her as she was ninety-four at the time, was not able to drive, and was unable to live alone any longer. "Granna," as we called her, was in the delivery room the day Danica came into the world. I distinctly remember her coming up alongside of me as I held this perfect, brand-new baby girl in my arms and saying, "Oh boy, we're gonna have fun now!" I have a picture of that moment where Granna had a clenched fist in the air as if to say, "Yes!"

Granna held Danica almost every day for the first few years of her life and then enjoyed reading to her and teaching her everything there was to know about the world every day after that. They had a very special bond because of those years together. By this time, the boys were ages three, six, and nine and were off and running. They didn't have much interest in sitting on Granna's lap listening to *Winnie the Pooh* stories anymore.

Granna was just one treasured part of our family. Mark and I are fortunate to have both sets of parents here in Flagstaff, and all of our siblings and their families nearby, some nearly in our backyard! There is never a shortage of family gatherings: a birthday party, a graduation, a barbeque, a football game, a shared ride to school, or a Sunday afternoon meal.

The Fire Department was like another extension of our family. We raised our kids together, attended barbeques, and spent Thanksgiving Day together when our husbands were on duty. Our kids sat on Santa's lap together at Christmas time and we watched fireworks every Fourth of July from the top of the training tower. Now that we are older, we are watching high school football games, sending kids off to college, and attending retirement parties.

From the outside looking in, life was moving along and was seemingly "perfect." We were building a life together and felt blessed beyond measure. We both had jobs that we enjoyed, and I was able to work part-time and be home most of the time with our precious children. We attended a solid church where I was leading women's ministry, our parents were nearby, we had a great home in the mountains, and we had friends galore. Life was good.

Christmas is the best time of year at the Wilson house. We begin the season as soon as December arrives by pulling out all of the red boxes and plastic containers from the attic, playing Christmas music for the first time, watching Christmas movies, and decorating the house. Finding our tree on December first had always been a tradition for our family, but it took on an entirely new meaning and tradition when Granna moved in with us. Instead of having to figure out what to get all of us for Christmas and then planning for someone to take her shopping, she decided to buy our Christmas tree each year. We have always enjoyed having a big, live tree, but I will never forget the first year she handed us a blank check and said, "I want you to go find the biggest, *best* tree you can find."

That evening, we all bundled up in our winter coats, hats, and gloves, and made a big thermos of hot chocolate. We drove to our favorite Christmas tree lot just down the road. The kids had already spent the last week eyeballing a giant noble fir leaning against the fence in the corner near the road. After a short drive, Mark helped Granna get out of the truck, and she enjoyed looking around the tree lot with us. It wasn't long before we all headed for the big one, like moths drawn to the porch light in summer. Granna had gotten cold and was now watching from inside the warm cab of the truck as we made out the check and the tree lot employees dragged our snow-covered tree across the lot. After Mark and the boys somehow managed to load and strap the giant fifteen-foot-tall fir to the trailer, we slowly drove home, sipping the last of our hot chocolate along the way.

It is always a feat getting the tree through the doorway and firmly planted in the steel tree base. Danica and I typically rearrange the living room and move things that might get broken as the giant tree makes its way into the house. It takes a group effort to make sure it is perfectly centered in its heavy-duty metal stand. Mark and the boys, with ladders on either side, hand the string of lights back and forth until the tree is completely covered in tiny white lights (my personal favorite) and small colorful lights (the kids' favorite). We then wander around the house turning off every light we can find to make sure there are no gaps without lights.

The tree looked perfect. Granna slowly, carefully unwrapped the crystal star she bought for us that first year and placed the first ornament right in the middle of the tree as we stood back and watched. Casting Crown's Christmas album played quietly in the background as we worked together to place the rest of the ornaments on the tree. It took a good while to carefully unwrap each Precious Moments and Hallmark ornament from different occasions in our lives. Special handmade elementary school ornaments and treasures from some of our favorite vacations sparked old memories. Granna would typically go back to her apartment to get ready for bed as we put the finishing touches on the tree. We truly did find the biggest tree that year and have carried on the tradition ever since. We treasure the years we had with Granna and especially the eight years and the priceless Christmases we were able to celebrate with her in our home. Granna went to be with Jesus on June 18, 2013, during a time when I was nearly too sick to grieve.

We still hang Granna's ornament first before anything else goes on the tree.

Christmas of 2012 began like any other. There was some snow on the ground outside, but our house was toasty warm. Mark and I had been up that morning for about an hour waiting for the magical moment when one of the kids would wake up and pry everyone else out of bed. At around seven o'clock, we finally watched four messy-haired sleepyheads wander out of their rooms in their new Christmas Eve pajamas. They would always come into the living room together to look in their stockings and to see how many cookies had been eaten and what kind of mess Santa had left by the fireplace. The younger ones would run out the front door to see if the reindeer, in fact, had eaten the carrots and oatmeal they had carefully spread out the night before. The video camera was turned on and in place and was loaded with new batteries, and a trash bag for paper and bows was hanging on the back door handle. We drank hot apple cider and snacked on breakfast pizza with Canadian bacon, hash browns, and eggs that I had prepared at midnight the night before. Mark read the true story of Christmas from the book of Luke, and we talked about the real meaning of Christmas. The next few hours were spent enjoying our lazy morning together, celebrating the birth of our Savior, sharing gifts, and creating cherished family memories.

The presents were unwrapped and the living room was a complete disaster. There were bags of trash, new clothes and gifts, and wadded up wrapping paper everywhere. Random red and green bows dotted the floor. Avery had given me a handmade book that year on colored paper with a "Free Neck Massage" coupon in it. Of course, I asked if I could use my coupon right away, and he went to work.

"Mom, what is this lump?"

To be honest, I hadn't noticed it before, but I reached up and felt the right side of my neck to find a fairly large lump. Mark said he had noticed a little lump a couple weeks before, but hadn't thought much of it because my neck has always been tight and full of knots (pretty lumpy, actually). It obviously had grown since then. We didn't think much of it at the time, but after a later discussion, decided I should at least make an appointment to have a doctor look at it. No big deal. I knew there was nothing to worry about.

I have been fairly healthy for most of my life and didn't have a primary care physician at the time, so I decided I'd better make an appointment with a nurse practitioner I had seen once before. After a general exam a couple weeks later, he felt that I was generally healthy, but after feeling the lump (which had already grown in size by this time), he recommended blood work and an x-ray just to "cover the bases." I wasn't very concerned, but felt that I should be cautious. I wasn't thinking much about the lump in my neck; I was still thinking about Christmas.

Thankfully, all of the tests came back normal. I specifically remember getting the official phone call to tell me the test results. I was sitting in my car just about to head in to see one of my young speech/language therapy clients when my cell phone rang. I remember the words so clearly: "Everything came back normal and it is probably just a *funky* lymph node…it's nothing we need to worry about. It's not cancer, so let's just keep our eye on it." When I should have been celebrating and jumping for joy, I hung up the phone with an overwhelming sense that something was wrong. In that moment, I knew in my heart that it was something serious. I can't take any credit for that. Some people call it a gut feeling, some call it instinct or intuition, but I knew this message was clearly from the sovereign God of the universe.

I knew it was bad.

It is no coincidence that my mom and dad had taken Granna (now 101 years old) to see an ear, nose, and throat (ENT) doctor for a routine visit about her ears earlier that same week. My mom remained in the exam room with Granna to make sure she had heard everything the doctor said, and she told him about the lump in my neck. We still laugh at the doctor's response: "Tell her to get her butt in here right now!" I thank God again and again that the doctor had such a great sense of urgency to see me. If I remember correctly, my mom told me what he said, and I called his office within a day or two. Dr. Nate Tritle was able to see me the following week, which is a miracle in and of itself given his very busy office and surgery schedule.

By the time Mark and I got in to Dr. Tritle's office, we had done some research on the Internet about possible causes of the lump (now bigger still and rapidly moving up toward my ear and toward the middle of my neck). We had narrowed it down in our simple minds to either some kind of infection in my lymph nodes or lymphoma. We had researched lymphoma a little and found out that although it is a scary diagnosis, it is quite treatable and very curable. Our hopes, of course, were that it was a simple infection that could be treated with a strong course of antibiotics. I still had no symptoms—only a harmless lump.

These kind of appointments are always nerve-racking. The minutes waiting in the exam room passed by so slowly, and I remember Mark and I trying to talk about anything else we could to pass the time and to stay distracted from the real reason we were there. The doctor came in shortly and listened as we explained our concerns. We presented our suspicions of lymphoma or a weird infection as if we knew what we were talking about. Doctors probably get a kick out of listening to their patients diagnose themselves. Doctor Tritle didn't waste any time. He promptly felt the growing lump in my neck and said we needed a biopsy right away. I had assumed he would recommend a biopsy, so I wasn't too surprised. I was surprised, however, with his rather intense sense of urgency. He wanted to perform the biopsy right away, meaning that same day.

What?

What was the rush?

I tried to explain to him that Mark and Avery were leaving that night (around 2:00 a.m.) for a much-anticipated fishing trip to Mexico and asked if we could schedule the biopsy for next week sometime. My common sense thinking was that the lump had probably been there for several weeks already; why not wait a few more days so the boys could take their trip?

Needless to say, I was fighting a losing battle. Instead of scheduling the biopsy after the weekend, Doctor Tritle cleared his calendar and scheduled me for a biopsy that evening. Although it was sudden, I was okay with that. I was still thinking, "Get the biopsy done, then let the boys go on their fishing trip since we won't have results until next week anyway." The news of my surgery traveled fast, and we were joined that evening by my parents, my brother, my best friend, Anita, and a good friend of my dad's who came to pray for me. I went in for a simple procedure of removing one of the enlarged lymph nodes on the right side of my neck. Doctor Nate Tritle's initials were drawn on my skin with a black Sharpie where the incision was to be made. I didn't know what kind of emotions or conversations were going on in the waiting room during this time, but I will never forget slowly waking up from anesthesia to Doctor Tritle's intense face. I remember hearing the words,

"cancer"…"carcinoma"…"unknown"…and that was about it.

Still groggy from anesthesia but alert enough to know at that moment that this was terrible news, I think I said, "Dang it!" and started to cry. For some reason, all I could think about was that Mark and Avery weren't going on their trip. I honestly think I was more brokenhearted about ruining their Mexico trip in that moment than hearing the cancer news. The next couple of hours were a blur. I don't remember getting dressed or getting into the car and I don't remember much about the ride home.

How do you tell your children that you have cancer?

What do you say?

How do you prepare them for what is to come when you don't even know what that is?

Because my biopsy was scheduled in the evening, Mark's parents had graciously offered to keep the kids for dinner and let the younger two spend the night if they wanted. This would make things easier since we wouldn't be home before bedtime. Kyle and Avery had eaten dinner and decided to head home so they could sleep in their own beds. Avery wanted to get to sleep because he was leaving on his Mexico fishing trip with Dad just a few hours later. Carter and Danica were already asleep at Grandma and Grandpa's house.

After a somber conversation on the way home, Mark and I agreed that we would wake Kyle and Avery up and tell them the news and that we would tell the other two in the morning. The dreaded task of telling our kids is still absolutely vivid to me. I waited in the living room downstairs as Mark went up to wake the boys. I couldn't sit down. I couldn't pray. I couldn't breathe.

I was standing in the living room, leaning on the large log post at the bottom of our stairs with tears running down my face when Mark and the sleepy-eyed boys walked into the room. Kyle didn't come all the way into the room but stood near the TV with his shoulder leaning on our big brick fireplace. Avery sat down on the brick hearth with a look of complete confusion on his face. As Mark began to talk, Kyle covered his mouth with one hand with his elbow resting in his other hand that was at his waist. His penetrating brown eyes were intense and he looked terrified. I had never seen a look like that on Kyle's face before. We could hear a weird sound that was difficult to identify at first. After a few minutes, we realized that we could actually hear Kyle's body reacting to this highly stressful, scary situation by releasing acid into his stomach throughout the conversation. The strange sound became louder and louder as the information came. Tears were streaming down Avery's face before Mark even began to speak. His eyes were full of fear, worry, disbelief, and probably even some anger. Not only did he just find out that his mom had cancer, but he was quickly realizing that his special trip with Dad was off. Poor guy! After hearing the news, Kyle left the room and went right to the computer that was set up in the dining room. Initially, we thought of stopping him, but realized that he needed to be able to communicate what was going on in his life to his friends as quickly as possible because he was hurting and afraid. This was a raw moment.

"Worst night of your life: when the strongest man you know is crying and telling you that your mom has cancer."

Chapter 3

Uncertainty

That was a long night—one that is etched on my soul forever. We spent several hours in the living room talking with the boys and crying. We agonized over telling the younger two, worrying about how much we would tell them and what we would say. Kids are smart and see right through our words sometimes. They see the look in our eyes, they hear us whispering and they know when something bad is happening.

Carter and Danica were able to get a good night's sleep at Grandma's before hearing the terrible news about their mama. We were up most of the night, but morning simply came too quickly. Mark drove over to his mom's early the next morning to pick the kids up. Grandma had fed them breakfast but they were still in their pajamas. Mark put them in the truck like he always does and then drove down the road in the opposite direction of our house as he told them what was happening. About thirty minutes passed before I heard the faint sounds of the truck pulling into the driveway. My heart was breaking. I wanted to run. I did not want to see the same fear and worry in their eyes, and I knew it was inevitable. Our big, wooden front door slowly swung open and two visibly troubled, heartbroken, and scared kids ran to me crying. Our family of six took the day off and spent the entire day at home, mostly in the living room where we held each other and cried. We were not prepared for this moment, and none of us were sure what our lives were going to look like from here.

What is it that a child clings to in times like these?

Each of our four children is a precious gift from God, and each one has such a uniquely different personality. They each dealt with this very scary and difficult time in their lives in a completely different way.

We have tried really hard to teach our children that they were uniquely created by God for a purpose that only He can fulfill. I have reminded them over and over that they were created with the same care and precision that God used to create the universe and that their lives are like picture frames where God can display His glory with the specific personalities, interests, looks, talents, and gifts He has given them (I loved this when I first read it in Stormie Omartian's *Power of a Praying Parent* book). A printed, framed version of this prayer is displayed in each of their bathrooms. We continue to work to instill in them Christ-like character qualities and traits and have done our best to "train them up in the way they should go." I am confident that this period of trial in their lives was also a part of God's sovereign plan that He would use to mold and shape them into who He wants them to be, and He will use this trial in their lives for His glory, and for their good. How that really plays out in real life, I'm not exactly sure.

Being the first-born and the oldest of our children, Kyle was a happy baby who grew into an independent, rather strong-willed child by the age of three. He is the one who, at the age of three, laid down at the end of the driveway with his chin resting on his hands, staring defiantly into his daddy's eyes and refused to come back home. He is a very smart young man who does well in school when he applies himself, and he is a natural, talented athlete. He loves to compete and he especially loves to *win* (don't we all?). Kyle has tried several different sports over the years, but had settled into baseball and football by around the eighth grade. He is a pitcher and a third baseman and was also the quarterback for his high school football team. He also enjoys hunting big game animals and birds and is rarely home because he wants to be wherever "the action" is. He is not big on communication and tends to internalize his emotions. I wondered how he would work through his fears and worries if he chose not to talk about them. Kyle spent his first two years of college on a full-ride baseball scholarship at an Arizona junior college. He will soon be a college senior, in Arkansas on a continued full baseball scholarship. Kyle had just turned seventeen and was a junior in high school when cancer showed up on our doorstep.

Avery is almost like a middle child with brothers on either side. He used to be involved in everything, but has recently developed a few more focused areas of interest. He is the musician and performer of the family. Avery first sang "Away in a Manger" at the age of three in front of our entire church and wasn't nervous at all. He has done multiple piano recitals and play performances, and is now comfortable running high school pep assemblies and leading worship at church. He stays on top of his academics and prefers to stay home more than go out. School comes fairly easy for him, and he is often asked to help the teacher in classes like chemistry. He was the president of his junior class and is an athlete (also baseball and football), a guitar player, a worship leader, and a cowboy. He is passionate about bass fishing, hunting, and working on a nearby ranch. He shows his emotions and enjoys talking. We are excited to see what career he chooses. He has had a longtime interest in medicine and has been accepted to Northern Arizona University on a full-ride academic scholarship. Avery was thirteen and in the eighth grade at a charter school when cancer showed up on our doorstep.

Carter will probably be designing, building, or working on something mechanical when he grows up. He loves anything with a motor and can identify the make of a vehicle from miles away. He is great with his hands and is the one who found the right tools to take off his training wheels at the age of two. We call on Carter to fix anything electronic or with a motor, and at the same time, he enjoys baseball, football, wrestling, hunting, and fishing. Carter wants to do things well, can be easily stressed at times, yet was the class president for two years at his middle school. He does everything with intensity (this is the child who has fallen into a twelve-foot hole, swallowed a bullet, and has already broken five bones!). Carter is in his first year of high school where he has enjoyed football and baseball and is looking forward to getting his first real job. Carter was ten and in fifth grade when cancer showed up on our doorstep.

As the baby of the family, and the only girl, Danica was born with a lot to say and has been a lovely and exciting addition to our house full of boys. She is the one who could memorize a story after it was read to her only one time and is also the one who memorized the Pledge of Allegiance before she was two. Danica has enjoyed soccer, t-ball, gymnastics, and now softball, volleyball and barrel racing. She loves school, loves to play and pretend, loves animals (especially horses), enjoys writing in journals, and is a great reader. She loves to play with her friends and she especially enjoys putting on shows or making music videos for the family. Our little Danica was only seven and in the second grade when cancer showed up on our doorstep. I wondered how cancer would impact our little girl who so desperately needed her mama?

I consider myself blessed beyond measure to be called "Mom" by these four amazing children. I remember dreaming of being a mom when I was a little girl. When I thought about growing up, I didn't think about where I would live or what kind of job I would have, but how many kids I would have and how we would spend our days.

I often thought back to my childhood years in Portland where Paul and I played all afternoon. Our modest forest green house on Bell Drive became the "hub" for all of the neighborhood children. Paul and I rode around on a go-kart he and my dad had built with a lawn mower motor, our parents helped us hold haunted houses in our basement, and we played endless games of hide and seek every evening until dark. We did carnivals and cake walks at our elementary school, I was a Blue Bird and Paul was a Cub Scout, and he played on a little league team. There was a small window of time when we were latchkey kids on an occasional day after school because of my mom's work schedule and my dad's classes, but we loved it. We got to eat sugary cereal right from the small cardboard boxes they came in just by tearing them open and dumping in the milk. There seemed to be something magical about those tiny boxes of Sugar Smacks. Time went by as we worked on mindless crafts and listened to music by Stevie Wonder, John Denver, the Osmonds, and Captain & Tennille. I memorized all the words to "Please Mister Postman" by the Carpenters and Simon & Garfunkel's "Mrs. Robinson." Life was good and being a kid was a blast. I wanted that same happy childhood for my kids.

There really has been no greater joy for me than being a mom to my own four children. I have spent countless hours on my knees for my children. I have prayed for them as they sleep that they would grow up to know who Jesus is and that I would be allowed to shepherd and minister to their tender hearts. I have prayed for their protection, their health, and for their life-long relationships with each other and with us. I have prayed for their friends, teachers, and future spouses. But suddenly, everything I had dreamed of and planned for was uncertain, to say the least. I could no longer see the future. I didn't know what cancer would mean for me as a wife and a mom. These thoughts swirled around in my head, but I tried to keep it inside. I knew in my heart that God was in control of my future, but I was wrestling with the reality that I may not be around for my family. My kids might receive their high school diplomas while grieving the loss of their mom. They might walk down the aisle someday and pass an empty chair in the front row meant for me.

None of us were sure what our lives were going to look like after this moment.

Chapter 4

Next Steps

I have cancer.

What do I do now?

What is the recommended treatment?

Do we even know what kind of cancer I have?

Where did it come from?

Will it spread?

Where do I get treatments?

Can my cancer be cured?

What about my kids?

Am I going to die and leave my children without a mama?

The questions in my head were endless, and the emotions were completely exhausting. I was trying to balance an overwhelming amount of new information, and I wasn't really able to think about much else. It was the first thing I thought of in the morning and the last thing I thought of before I went to sleep. I woke up all night long and thought about it some more. In an instant, I was forced to wrestle with my own mortality. I tried to sort out all of the information people were giving me, and believe me, there was a lot. I think it took a little while to even begin to accept the word *cancer*. I just remember feeling confused and completely lost most of the time.

The radiation/oncology doctor's words to me in one of our first appointments replay in my head as if they were uttered yesterday. It had already been a long, grueling day with doctors and nurses overloading us with details of the horrendous treatment regimen to come and all of its possible side effects. Few people can handle hearing all of this information at once, and clearly I wasn't one of them. I was doing my best to process every detail, one at a time, but it was all coming so fast. We were told we should stay in Phoenix, and the doctor described how much we would have to be away from home. We were told it would get harder and harder on my body to make the trip. I clearly remember being told, "You will just have to put being a mom on hold for a bit." This was a raw, tender moment that nearly broke my heart. I didn't expect those harsh words to hit me so hard and wasn't exactly sure what the doctor meant. My eyes filled with tears instantly, and I blurted out something uncontrollable like, "I don't think you understand...being a mom is who I am and what I do...I can't just put being a mom on hold."

So begins the next phase of our journey.

Mark and I began anxiously trying to gather information about my new diagnosis so that we could make the most educated decisions possible. We quickly realized we knew absolutely nothing about anything. Everywhere we went in our beautiful, small, mountain town, we were swarmed by crowds of people who knew and loved us, which was lovely yet emotionally draining. They wanted to know the plan and wanted to help, but we didn't really even know at this point what kind of help we might need. All I could do was cry. I remember so many of our sweet friends putting their arms around me and crying right along with me. They didn't know what to do either. It seemed as if our entire town was just as sad and as scared as we were. That was comforting in a weird sort of way, and also alarming. I felt as if I had been given a death sentence and everybody knew it, but no one wanted to say it out loud.

We were graciously offered countless perspectives on how we should go about treatment; where we should go, who we should see, who we should not see. Books were dropped off on our front porch and handed to us at church. Books from Amazon arrived in the mailbox. Books about cancer, books about suffering and death, books both for and against chemotherapy, books about natural treatments and diet supplements. Bags and bags of books. We received countless texts and emails from friends who sent us links to various websites full of information about cancer, cancer centers, and treatment options. More books. I was initially overwhelmed by so much information, the hugely vast variety of information, and everyone's different opinions and expectations. As we talked and sorted through information, we prayed for wisdom and discernment outside of ourselves because it was just too much.

Meanwhile, God was putting a plan together.

One of Mark's longtime friends and fellow Fire Department co-workers Dave had been successfully treated for a throat cancer several years prior by a renowned ENT named Dr. Michael Hinni at the Mayo Clinic in Scottsdale, which was about 150 miles away. Dr. Hinni is a graduate of the University Of Missouri School Of Medicine with more than twenty-seven years of extensive experience with throat cancer and head/neck surgery. He had surgically removed all of Dave's cancer without subsequent radiation or chemotherapy, and Dave is thankfully cancer free to this day. Both Dave and his wife were adamant that we should see Dr. Hinni and absolutely no one else.

Some people thought we needed to stay in Flagstaff. What should we do? We weren't sure if the Mayo Clinic even accepted our insurance at this point. All we knew is that we wanted the absolute best doctors and team of professionals we could find. We were, after all, talking about my head and neck here, not just my big toe! It wasn't long before we learned that the Mayo Clinic had only recently begun (within the last year) accepting our specific insurance. Amazing! We prayed fervently that God would make the best plan known to us—and He did. Information was beginning to come together, and Mark and I felt God leading us to the Mayo Clinic. It became overwhelmingly clear, and we had a sense of peace about where I would receive medical care. Mark only recently told me that my dad took him aside one day and firmly told him he had better get me the absolute best care there was. He and my mom were worried about their little girl.

In the first part of February I had an introductory appointment with Dr. Hinni who conducted some additional tests to try and locate the source of origin of the cancer spreading in my neck. He was convinced he would find it. Up to this point, it was "unknown." I wasn't exactly sure what that meant, although I could tell from the way all of the medical people said "unknown primary" that it couldn't be good. I eventually learned that it would be difficult to treat my cancer if they didn't know exactly where it was coming from. That made sense. Mark and I were surprised to see that Dr. Hinni had a similar sense of urgency as did Dr. Tritle in Flagstaff. He was intrigued and committed to finding the source. He pushed his medical team to get things moving forward as soon as possible due to the location of the cancer and the aggressive metastasis in the lymph nodes on the right side of my neck.

Aggressive metastasis.

What exactly does that mean?

I remember the elevator door opening after we pushed the button on one of our early visits to the Mayo Clinic. An elderly woman, I am guessing near eighty, stood inside cloaked in a pale blue hospital gown with a frail grip on her IV pole. I made brief eye contact with her as Mark and I entered, but quickly looked away. Trying to be as discreet as possible, I realized she had a gaping hole in her face where the tip of her nose and left nostril used to be. My heart literally ached, and I almost felt nauseous as I thought of the drastic surgery she must have had and how it was likely cancer that changed her life and appearance forever. Knowing I had an aggressive cancer growing somewhere in my head and neck was not a comforting thought at this point, and I was racked with fear. We soon reached our floor and stepped out of the elevator for the next appointment.

Breathe.

I could hear doctors and nurses talking about me, about cancer. Surgeries, treatments, timelines. I didn't understand most of what I was hearing, but I could tell that everyone was very concerned. I would try to listen to their clinical opinions and explanations, but much of it went in one ear and out the other. I was in a fog. The dark clouds were moving in quickly, and I was terrified. So much to process, so many changes—and so fast! Within a couple of weeks, an extremely detailed, rigorous plan was put in place to find and treat this aggressive cancer that was growing inside of me.

Our sovereign God was lining up all of the details so that things moved rather quickly. There were times when things moved so fast, I felt as if I were unable to breathe. I could do nothing. I was completely relying on and forced to trust people I had never met to figure this out and save my life.

After multiple "exploratory" appointments and additional MRIs, I was scheduled for a radical neck dissection by Dr. Hinni. Just the words "radical neck dissection" were disturbing. He was certain that he would find the source of my cancer during this intense surgery where he would remove all of the lymph nodes on the right side of my neck, along with taking out both tonsils, a portion of the base of my tongue and snipping away at other areas of suspicion like the back wall of my throat. The surgery sounded quite invasive and possibly debilitating, but the doctor boasted that I would leave the operating room cancer-free. Mark and I definitely liked his level of confidence. Given all of the uncertainty about the origin of my cancer and what would happen next, his words sounded pretty positive. Cancer-free. I couldn't argue with that.

As I was being prepped for this massive, invasive surgery, Dr. Hinni came up to my bedside to inform me that the team had met one more time to brainstorm over a new set of imaging results. After hours of study and discussion, they had found the source of my cancer on the posterior pharyngeal wall behind my nose and throat. They were able to see a thickened area of the mucosal lining where the cancer had decided to rear its ugly head. More importantly, they found another cancerous lymph node behind that back wall of my nose and throat on the brain side, very near a major artery at the base of my brain. Cancer; stage four. Surgery was no longer a viable option, and the only hope for treatment was radiation and chemotherapy. I would later be thankful to have avoided the massive neck dissection, but not at this moment.

Stage four cancer?

Chemotherapy?

The very word resonated into the depths of my soul in that moment. I had really hoped to avoid chemo, and I cried at the mere mention of the word. At the time, the surgery seemed like more of an instant fix, and I knew that radiation with chemo would be a long, difficult road…at least I thought I did. I also remember thinking about throwing up and losing my long, blonde hair. I didn't really understand what radiation meant at that point, so I don't remember thinking about that part too much. Chemo was enough. Looking back now, I am so grateful that God directed the team to find the primary source of my cancer and that He kept me off of the operating table. I later learned that a radical neck dissection involves not only removal of all the lymph nodes on the affected side of the neck, but it could include removal of the spinal accessory nerve, internal jugular vein, and the sternocleidomastoid muscle. Needless to say, it is an intense, complicated procedure, and would have likely left me quite disfigured. God had a very different treatment path in mind for me, but the mention of chemo and radiation was my first inclination that this was going to be a marathon, not a quick sprint. I had some idea of what my treatment was going to take—what it would take from me and also take away from me—but I had no way of knowing what it would give me in return.

February 27 (Laura; just before my forty-fifth birthday):

> Treatment plans unfold: We were at the Mayo Clinic for a couple of appointments. All went well and they did a "simulator" to get me ready for radiation therapy. We will have to go down again a day or two next week for additional appointments and preparation, but it sounds like the official start date will not be until the eleventh. I will have my first radiation treatment that day, as well as my first dose of chemo. They said it would be a long day and to just plan on spending the night in Phoenix. Our hope is that I will have my second radiation treatment Tuesday morning and then head home to be with the kiddos. We want to do some down-and-back trips in the beginning if we can, but we will have to see how it all works out.
>
> Please continue to pray, as we get ready to start this process, that we can run this race in a way that honors our Savior, that we are able to drive back and forth as much as possible in the beginning; that we do not get consumed by fear; that our family (especially our children) will

be comforted through all of this; that the radiation therapists will be precise in their treatment; that the Lord protects my swallow mechanism, salivary glands, and taste buds from the radiation as much as possible; and, of course, that this cancer is knocked out quickly and completely!

March 3 (Laura):

One More Week of "Normal": Keep praying as we prepare for next week—only one more week of "normal." We should be going to the Mayo this week to have the port put in and for a few "prep" appointments prior to starting treatments. They should contact us tomorrow with the specific schedule. We have been told that we will have to spend Monday nights in Phoenix because Mondays will be long and difficult days, getting both radiation and chemo. Thank you again for all of your encouragement, love, support, and especially your prayers!

CHAPTER 5

Who has Time for Cancer?

March 6 (Laura):

Schedules are being set and details are coming together.
Mark and I are heading to Phoenix tonight (after watching
Kyle's baseball game) for a full day of appointments
tomorrow (from insurance/payment meetings to hearing
tests, consultations with doctors, and chemotherapy
education). Friday at one thirty, they will put in what
they call a "power-port," where I will receive the chemo
treatments as well as all kinds of other medications/
IV fluids/etc. along the way. They said to expect to be
released after this minor surgery around four., so we plan
to be back home Friday evening. It sounds like we are still
on track for starting everything on Monday, but they are
still "hammering out" some of the scheduling details.

March 8 (Laura):

The power port was put in without complication, and the
surgeon was able to place it on my left side so that it didn't
interfere with the cancerous lymph nodes on the right
side. (This was a blessing at the time, although it ended
up being in an uncomfortable place for my seatbelt to rest

while driving later). We now had an official schedule for the coming seven weeks of daily radiation. At this point, we planned to spend time with our children at home on Monday mornings and see them off to school before getting in the car for the two-hour drive to the Mayo Clinic Radiation/Oncology Department.

Things were happening so fast! I remember vividly being at home alone one day. I was emotionally exhausted. I wasn't sleeping well. I wasn't eating well. I had been trying to hold it in, but I felt my emotions looking for an escape route. I knew I was the only one home and I very purposely walked into my bedroom and closed the door. There, at the end of myself, the floodgates opened and I began to cry. The crying intensified. I wept. I sobbed. I bawled. I remember my entire body going limp in that moment. I fell to my knees and screamed, "*Nooooo!*" as loud as I could. My spirit crumbled that day as the emotion poured in and completely took over. I was alone with my grief, with my fear...with the unknown. I literally lay curled up in the fetal position on my bedroom floor. It didn't last long, but all of the emotion that had been building up inside of me for the past few weeks finally had to make its way out. I am just thankful nobody was home.

We settled into spending most Monday nights in Phoenix so that we could be there for the Tuesday early morning blood draw and radiation treatment, followed by six long hours of chemotherapy infusions. The day started and ended hard. Just walking into the Mayo Clinic was hard. There were sick, hurting people everywhere and most of them were considerably older than me. I would receive confused looks and glances at times, mostly because I didn't look sick. Yet.

We were constantly amazed at the powerful hand of God in the scheduling details. The nurses and doctors all worked with us so that we could be home with our children as much as possible. I tried to be positive, but I absolutely hated being away from the kids. We went back and forth to Phoenix a lot for the next several months but always managed to make it home when the kids needed us the most.

By the beginning of April, our kids were settling into their new weekly schedule with us being gone two nights a week. Their mama, who looked and acted healthy for as long as they could remember, was suddenly sick and in a battle against something ugly, unknown, uncertain, and incredibly powerful. Mark and I will probably never fully know how difficult this time was on each of them. I continue to pray that they can talk openly about it and share their struggles, emotions, and experiences with us.

Mark and I felt like strangers in a foreign land those first few weeks. Walking through the doors of the Mayo Clinic as a patient isn't fun for anyone. It made me feel sicker by just being there. We could feel the looks of strangers, some of pity and some of wonder. Patients in the big waiting room were in varied states: some were thin and frail, some still had hair, and others were covered in a scarf or soft hat. Some appeared happy and others looked broken. Still others were asleep.

Before beginning treatment, the radiation oncologist began planning my intense therapy regimen. I also met with an oncologist who was planning the chemo therapy part of my treatment. I would be receiving chemo once a week during my daily radiation treatments and another course of chemo later in the summer. I was told I had to see my dentist prior to starting radiation to make sure there were no problems with my teeth. Many people require dental work prior to starting radiation and often have teeth removed. Fortunately, I had a clear checkup. No decay, no cavities, and no loose fillings. Rubber mouth guards were made for both my top and bottom teeth to prevent any metal fillings from deflecting the radiation rays.

Next, I had an appointment with the Mayo speech/language pathologist to evaluate my swallowing ability. Being a speech/language pathologist myself, I was becoming very aware of the importance of swallowing exercises I would need to do throughout my treatment in order to keep my swallowing muscles active and strong. This was an area I had studied extensively and specialized in. I had taught graduate level courses on normal and disordered swallowing. Suddenly, I was the patient and my ability to swallow was on the line. This was tough. I thought I knew what I needed to do, but what I didn't realize is that my swallowing could become "difficult" as treatment progressed and possibly for a lifetime. I wasn't exactly sure what that would mean, but I wanted to do everything I could to preserve function as long as possible. I was also told that most patients receiving radiation to the head and neck require a feeding tube at some point because of the harsh impacts to the swallowing mechanism. Not me. I was determined that I could do enough swallowing exercises and force myself to swallow so that I could avoid this.

I met with a dietician who tried to prepare me for what was to come. She was a compassionate young woman with brown, curly hair, and it was evident right away that she loved the Lord as I do. We had an instant connection, although I swore to loathe her for all of eternity when she spoke of the feeding tube (you know who you are). She talked to Mark and I about all it would take to meet my nutritional needs as treatment progressed and side effects worsened. I tried to tune her out, to be honest. I didn't want to hear about fat grams and protein shakes! Thankfully, Mark was paying attention and writing things down.

Following my appointment with the dietician, I had to meet with a gastroenterologist to discuss the likely placement of a feeding tube. Gross! Once again, I checked out. I was confident that I would be one of the few patients that would not need a feeding tube. I would force myself to eat no matter how bad things became.

CHAPTER 6

The Gift that Keeps on Giving

Some people want all the facts and every gory detail. That was Mark, the emergency manager. He wanted every bit of information that was out there so that he could be prepared for whatever medical situation might be coming. He appreciated having a former head and neck cancer patient share specific details with him about the journey ahead. He spent hours on the phone with a friend of my parents' who had gone through the same brutal radiation treatment for throat cancer. I remember Mark asked if he could put him on speakerphone several times while we were driving so I could hear. Definitely not. I adamantly refused, in fact, I purposely looked away so I didn't see the stress and worry building on Mark's face as the ugly details unfolded. He only recently told me that he pulled into an abandoned parking lot alone one day to focus on all of the negative information that had been shared with him and was completely overwhelmed by what was to come. I, on the other hand, did not want to know exactly how bad it was going to get. I knew I couldn't handle much more. My future was already scary and uncertain, and I knew the road ahead was going to be brutal. I didn't need any more details. In fact, I didn't really want any more negative information because I knew it would be more than I could process. I only wanted to hear what I absolutely needed in that moment. There is a reason the verse in Matthew 6:34 says, "Today has enough trouble of its own." I was processing things slowly and gradually, and only as I needed to. This was merely survival mode for me.

"You will be getting radiation therapy to your head and neck every day for seven weeks, five days a week, totaling thirty-five treatments."

The doctor continued, "A beam of radiation will be directed to the target areas in your nasopharynx, neck, and surrounding tissues from an arc radiation machine."

I remember having a very basic understanding that a beam of some kind would be entering my body and attacking the cancer cells, but I was taking in a lot of new and overwhelming information, so my comprehension was limited, to say the least. I really had no idea what that meant. I think I would hear the information on some level, but I was not really listening—probably a protective mechanism of some sort. I heard the doctors say that the effects of radiation tend to be cumulative and build on themselves. That is why the side effects keep increasing as treatment progresses. Radiation of my head and neck was obviously going to expose a lot of normal, non-cancerous tissue to the damaging radiation rays during treatment. In addition to all of the mouth and throat damage, I was told that the skin on my neck and face might become irritated or even burned. Some said my skin might start to look and feel sunburned.

The most common oral problems from radiation to the head and neck are mucositis, meaning inflammation of the mucous membranes of the mouth. Mouth sores are common, as are thrush and difficulty swallowing. The entire gastrointestinal tract, particularly the mouth and throat, can take a beating during radiation. In addition to mucositis, some patients have bleeding and infection in their mouth. Most patients battle thrush during and after their treatment. Injury to the parotid glands (the ones that house the salivary glands) from radiation to the head and neck can make swallowing a constant challenge. Sometimes, complications can be severe enough that treatment must be stopped. It can also lead to all kinds of dental problems because of poor oral moisture and severe damage from the radiation rays. Radiation to the head and neck also often causes fibrosis or scarring in the soft tissues of the neck and can damage the muscles and joints of the jaw. This was a lot to take in.

And then there was chemo. I had cried in that pre-op room where Dr. Hinni first said that terrifying word—and for good reason. Surgery and radiation are designed to remove, kill, or damage cancer cells, but chemo works throughout the entire body. It is a powerful medicine that can wreak all kinds of havoc. Many cancer patients experience physical, emotional, and mental exhaustion, as well as intestinal issues. I had heard of some who have had uncontrollable diarrhea or constipation or daily vomiting. Chemo can bring memory loss, hair changes, low red blood cell counts, fertility issues, and can even cause early or sudden menopause. I read somewhere that chemo can make you feel dead without having actually died. I remember trying to explain to Danica what chemo was going to do to her mama. The very drug designed to save my life would look like it was going to kill me. I came to a new understanding of what this meant when the side effects were at their most intense point for several weeks after I completed my seven weeks of radiation.

It sounds so simple, but this was one of the most brutal experiences of my life so far. I don't know if it is true, but several of my nurses and doctors said that the condition of my mouth and throat was one of the worst they had seen (maybe they were just trying to help me not feel like such a baby). I can attest that the severe inflammation and burns to the back of my mouth and throat literally burned my uvula off! For those non-speech pathology people, the uvula is that little piece of tissue that hangs down from the soft palate above the back of your tongue (in graduate school, we lovingly referred to it as the "hangy-down thingy"). I am sad to report that mine is now missing.

Many get dehydrated and suffer from malnutrition. Not me, thanks to Nurse Mark, who literally forced nutrients into my body.

Thrush was an unwelcomed and frequent visitor due to my weakened immune system and from the steroids I was receiving with my chemo. It often made its way all the way down my beat-up esophagus. Usually, thrush is treated with Nystatin, a lovely thick, yellow liquid that is swished around the mouth and then swallowed. It burned my mouth and throat terribly, and the texture made me gag. The mere mention of Nystatin now can almost bring me to tears.

CHAPTER 7

The "Dreaded Mask"

The first day of radiation was terrifying, to say the least. I opted not to wear a hospital gown. For some reason, wearing my own clothes was a big deal to me at the time. Looking back, I think it allowed me to feel like I was at least in control of one tiny little thing. I came to radiation each day in comfy yoga pants, the running shoes Mark and the kids had bought me for my birthday, and a soft cotton V-neck shirt. I took out my dangly earrings and was handed my previously made rubber mouth guards to protect my teeth from the harsh beams of radiation. I was asked to lie down and remain completely immobilized on the table. My arms and legs were strapped down next. I stared up at the ceiling. I remember at one point being asked if I were an anxious person, and I confidently said no. I was then asked if I was claustrophobic, and I said no. The stiff, white, plastic mask was then placed over my entire head, face, neck, and shoulders, and attached to the table.

"Oh wait—maybe I am anxious and claustrophobic! Please get this thing off of me!"

The "dreaded mask" is privileged to have its own chapter, as it has actually become a strange term of endearment. That stiff, plastic radiation mask was one of my least favorite things I have experienced in my lifetime thus far. It served to hold my head and neck in place so that the radiation beams could target the cancer cells specifically. So, in essence, the dreaded mask helped to save my life.

First in the process of radiation therapy treatment planning is the "radiation simulation." This involved positioning my body, making marks on my face and neck with a Sharpie, and taking imaging scans to line things up. To make the mask, the therapists placed a warm, wet sheet of plastic mesh over my face and then shaped it around my head, neck, and shoulders. The mask quickly hardened as it cooled and it was then fitted to my face with even more detail. This firm thermoplastic mask was now molded to fit my specific facial features, the curve of my nose and jawline, and my neck and shoulders. It was worn every day for thirty to forty minutes while the powerful and destructive radiation beams were directed specifically at the cancer lurking behind my nose and throat.

During the simulation, I was positioned on my back on a hard, cold table, my feet were strapped down to make sure I was still, and the mask was then fastened to the table.

There was no moving once my entire body was secured and still. Additional CT scans were then done to determine the exact locations where treatment would be focused. Radiation therapy is quite an amazing technology, although I still don't really understand how it all works. I do know that radiotherapy has to be aimed very precisely at its target, so I had to lie completely still for the entire treatment session. That is a difficult feat when your entire being is racked with fear and anxiety. The slightest movement could change where the radiation rays are aimed, as well as the precision and effectiveness of treatment. After the radiation simulation planning was finished, I was ready to begin radiation treatments the following Monday. I still didn't really know what to expect, even though there was no shortage of information given to me. I can only compare it to childbirth. No matter how many Lamaze classes you take or how many birthing books or videos you memorize, there is no way to truly know what to expect until your own labor pains begin.

I wanted to jump off the table and run out the door, but I couldn't. I couldn't move. My body was experiencing the automatic fight-or-flight response, but I couldn't do either. This was *not* a comfortable place to be.

One of the technicians placed a warm blanket over my legs. Oh, the joy of a blanket straight out of the warmer! I tried as hard as I could to focus on the blanket warming my icy skin. My mind was in overdrive and I was beginning to panic. My entire body was in a state of constant muscle contraction, I was shaking and sweating profusely, my heart was pounding. I had terrible cotton mouth and it felt like I couldn't swallow or breathe. All I could do was lie still on the hard, cold table. I tried to ignore the mask and look through the small holes. I could only see the ceiling, so I focused on the white tile squares and tried to pray. I could hear the faint voices of radiation technicians talking to each other as they skillfully operated the big machine behind the one-way mirror in the room next door. I heard the clicking sounds of the machines that were designed to save my life. This first thirty-minute session seemed to last for hours.

A new CT simulation was performed a week into treatment. After my normal radiation session, I was told I had to be fitted again. This procedure was done to make sure nothing had shifted in the mask placement and setup of the radiation computer imaging. So another twenty to thirty minutes in the mask— ugh! I say this lightly now, but I literally broke down and cried when they told me.

CHAPTER 8

Gripped by Fear

March 6 (Laura):

> Pray for me not to be afraid. I know that fear comes from
> the enemy and, although it is a normal response, I don't
> want to stay there. Some of you will remember me saying
> a few short weeks ago that I don't really struggle with fear
> and anxiety…it's almost funny now!

I was afraid of everything.

Afraid of cancer. Afraid of death. Afraid of the unknown. Afraid of
treatment and its effects. Afraid of throwing up from chemo and losing
my hair. Afraid of the mask and the possibility of a feeding tube. Afraid
for my family. I had absolutely no control over what was happening, and
fear was doing all it could to consume me.

I watched cancer treatment miraculously save my sweet mom's life
more than twenty years ago when she battled against a football-sized
fibrous histiocytoma that was taking over her left quadriceps muscle,
but I also watched it steal her appetite, her strength, her hair, and part
of her life. I really didn't want that. Not everyone diagnosed with cancer
has chemotherapy or radiation. Some are cured in other ways and others
have cancers that are sadly untreatable. No one knows exactly how
chemotherapy will affect them, and no words or description can truly do
it justice. It comes in many different forms and goes to work attacking

any and every cell that is busy dividing. We have a lot of body parts where normal cells are dividing, so chemo can affect all kinds of things during its unwelcome visit. Some side effects show up almost instantly and others are late bloomers. The idea is that the ugly side effects are temporary and will eventually go away after treatment ends. Unfortunately, some long-term changes decide to stay.

My chemo/oncology team at the Mayo was amazing. They were compassionate and tender and were often a source of great encouragement for me when I was afraid. As time went on, the struggle to stay awake intensified, and somehow I wasn't as afraid as much. I lay propped up on a bed while Mark sat in a comfy chair near me. My IV was placed first thing in the morning after blood work and radiation. Steroids were pushed in later, followed by much-needed potassium and anti-nausea medications. The awful poison came next and would take nearly all day to work its way through my body. In between trips to the Mayo cafeteria or coffee station, Mark would patiently sit and watch the life literally being sucked out of me as multiple chemo drugs went to work. He could always tell by the color of my skin and the look in my eyes when chemo took over. As the treatment continued, I was often blankly staring into space by mid-afternoon. After many long trips to the bathroom dragging my IV pole (commonly referred to as "George"), forcing myself to drink what seemed like gallons of water to help move the chemo through my liver and kidneys, and making myself eat a few bites of dry, tasteless cafeteria food while I still could, I took a few naps. On the days I could keep my eyes open, I tried to read. I so appreciated the privacy of my little "chemo suite" as the worsening treatment symptoms became more of a challenge. We requested this private space every week and it was available all but once. It had a sliding glass door that allowed us to pass the long hours talking, sleeping, or watching movies without bothering other patients nearby. We were usually done around 4:00 p.m. after more anti-nausea meds and steroids were pushed through my IV.

By the time we were making our way up the mountain from Phoenix on Friday afternoons, the harsh chemo that was forced into my body earlier that week was taking its toll. If the terrible fatigue, the weakness, and the achiness in my bones weren't enough, then there was "chemo brain." My diagnosis, along with my narcotic pain medications, had already thrown me into a fog of confusion. I didn't necessarily need the added fog that chemotherapy brought. I think I still have some of it, but my kids tell me now it's just my age.

I tried hard to fight the effects of treatment, but with the intense impacts of radiation, treatment seemed to be winning. Week by week, as the chemo cycles continued, I would find myself slipping into that heavy fog. The television was on more than normal and time passed agonizingly slow. I watched repeated episodes of *Chopped*, which is ironic given the fact that I couldn't eat a darn thing. I remember hearing the rhythm of the kitchen clock. Since I was receiving chemo infusions weekly, a pattern developed where Mark and I could predict fairly consistently how I would feel on a given day. The achiness and severe fatigue would slowly ease up and I would begin to feel a bit stronger over the weekend, just in time for it all to start again the following Monday. This had to have been hard on poor Mark. He was doing a lot of caring for me and carrying the enormous burden of the situation while still trying to be a husband and father. He was exhausted, afraid, overwhelmed, and probably feeling helpless at times. He was also doing all of the driving while I slept.

I am usually the one who stays awake on road trips. But, over time, those long drives from the Mayo Clinic back up the mountain into the pines were mostly spent with my eyes closed. I only remember one emergency stop for vomiting after receiving a new, heavy-duty pain medication; otherwise, I slept. It seems I would always wake up on the straight, flat stretch coming into town. When the peaks came into view, I knew we were almost home where I could be with the loves of my life for a couple days before starting the dreaded routine again.

When the cycle of chemotherapy comes to an end, it often takes a while before people begin to feel like themselves again. Sometimes weeks and for others, months. I had a long way to go, for sure. These painful experiences have helped me to see how very little I understood when my mom went through her cancer treatment. I wish I knew then what I know now so that I could have been more compassionate and helpful than I was twenty years ago. So sorry, Mama.

The first week of radiation treatments wearing the mask was

awful, and I constantly battled fear, worry, anxiety, panic attacks, and claustrophobia. Remember, I am not typically a nervous person. The daily treatments eventually got a little easier and a little more routine, but I repeatedly succumbed to doubt, anxiety, and fear.

I got to know my radiation/oncology therapists pretty well since I saw them almost every day. They were all so kind and caring and did what they could to make me as comfortable as possible. After a few days of radiation, I knew exactly how long each treatment session would last, and I would literally count the minutes. One of my sweet friends, Beth, whom I had known since I taught her in Pioneer Girls as a young girl, made me a new CD for each week of radiation. The first one was full of some of my favorite worship songs about trusting God in times of fear. Chris Tomlin's "Whom Shall I Fear?" was the first song on the CD. The radiation technicians knew to put it in the CD player on the counter and hit "play" just before my treatment started. They often asked me if it was loud enough, and a muffled "No! Louder, please!" came from beneath the white plastic mask. I tried to drown out all of the other noises in the room with worship music. These songs ministered to me so much. They helped to keep my mind focused on Christ and reminded me of His perfect power and sovereignty. I closed my eyes and pictured a literal army of angels surrounding me. I knew I had to, or I was going under. "Whom Shall I Fear?" became almost an anthem or a fight song for me during those radiation days, although a completely different set of feelings takes over now when I hear it played or sung in church. A flood of emotion hits as soon as I hear the first note. Then a negative association comes in and takes me right back under the mask. The negative eventually fades, and it doesn't take long for God to remind me of the gift He gave me in that song. Then I begin to cry. By the end of the song, I have probably gone through every one of my emotions. Thank you, Chris Tomlin, and thank you, Beth, for the gift of music. It was a shelter for me in the storm.

Chris Tomlin - Whom Shall I Fear (God of Angel Armies)

You hear me when I call
You are my morning song
Though darkness fills the night
It cannot hide the light

Whom shall I fear?

You crush the enemy underneath my feet
You are my Sword and Shield
Though troubles linger still

God was calling me to believe He was faithful even though I couldn't see it. I was struggling to believe the very things that I knew to be true. There were countless days I wept silently during those long moments under the mask. I wept because I knew I was weak. I wept because there was nothing I could do to fix this. I wept because I knew only God could.

CHAPTER 9

Good and Perfect Gifts

Even though our lives were dominated and nearly paralyzed by cancer and necessary treatment schedules, God still allowed room for our personalities and interests to shine. Danica was still doing gymnastics and the boys were in the middle of their baseball seasons. There were a lot of sporting events to attend, and somehow, as sick and weak as I was, I didn't want to miss anything if I didn't have to. Even as I spent many games wrapped in a blanket as my symptoms worsened, God gave me some special moments along the way.

A baseball game in Holbrook (a small town about ninety miles east of Flagstaff), when my diagnosis was fairly new, stands out. Kyle had pitched a great game and had just started his laps around the edge of the outfield to move the lactic acid out of his body. Without thinking, I asked his coach if I could run with him. I had never done that before and have never thought of it since, but for some reason I did that day. His coach said, "Sure!" and I joined Kyle on his next few laps. We shared a tender moment that windy day in Holbrook, and I feel as though God gave me a precious gift with my son on that field. Kyle would later pull away as cancer invaded our home.

Around the same time, Avery was playing on a travel baseball team, and we found ourselves in Phoenix for a weekend tournament. The sports complex had several fields adjacent to each other with a restaurant in the middle. As Mark, the kids, and I neared the field with our stadium chairs and snacks, we began to notice people glancing at us and looking back to the boys on the field and in the dugout. We soon realized that the entire team and some of the parents were wearing Nike sweatbands on their wrists bearing the initials "LW" and a heart. I did what I do best: I cried. I was still crying when all fifteen players in their navy blue and yellow uniforms formed a circle, removed their hats, took a knee, and prayed for me. I have a special photo of those boys in that moment that I will treasure forever.

Carter's Little League team, coached by Mark, won the City Championship that year, and I was miraculously able to be there for every nail-biting game. I was sick and frail by this time, but I was there. I was thrilled to be a part of the joy and pride that came with the win, t o witness the game-winning catch or the last strike. When the crazy fans ran out onto the field to celebrate, I took my twenty-four-hour chemo fanny pack and my fuzzy blanket and I went too.

There were a lot of joys during those days, and there were also some games that found me alone. I thought if I sat by myself, I could hide in some way and avoid the onslaught of difficult questions and conversations. Talking and smiling were challenging because of the severe mucositis, the mouth sores, and the lack of saliva. My appearance was also changing for the worse every day, and sometimes hiding was just plain easier.

Sports have been such a part of our lives that somehow they were never really allowed to take a backseat in our family. There were times that my treatment regime felt somewhat like training for a sport. Mark referred to offense and defense frequently during this time. Up until treatment was underway, we didn't feel like we could "attack" anything, we just had to sit back and wait for someone to put the plays together for us. Now that things were moving and we had a routine, it was game on (especially for Mark)!

March 11 (Laura):

> Another sports analogy—what can I say? We have a house full of athletes! Mark reminded us all today that this cancer has been on the offense for the past couple of months, and all we could do was remain on defense. Tomorrow, however, the Wilson family is taking offense

and is ready to fight! Please pray for our strength and endurance; it is going to be a long game! We know that many of you are on the sidelines and in the stands with us—keep praying! Pray specifically that our children are comforted this week and that I am not afraid during the radiation treatment; it is a little scary with everything being directed at my head and neck. Yikes! Also pray that I can tolerate the chemotherapy fairly well and that we can make the trip home Wednesday to be with our kiddos.

March 12 (Mark):

So as I write this, we are sitting in the room with pre-chemo infusions taking place. We are just realizing how fast our lives have changed. While it would be easy to focus on the negatives, the positives are all around us and are too great to ignore. God is so good to us in so many ways (large and small) and continues to go before us while always having our backs. Laura has successfully completed two radiation treatments and has taken the "Whom Shall I Fear?" song with her on CD (Thanks, Beth!). This song gives her the peace of knowing that while I am left standing at the door, God and His angel armies march right in before her and remain by her side the entire time. While she won't tell you the mask is enjoyable, He has given her the courage to endure it so far. With God as our solid rock, we know that while this will be a long journey with numerous storms along the way, we are assured of our foundation and will not be moved. Laura has had pain radiating from her right clavicle area down to her shoulder over the past several days when she breathes, and is sleeping upright in a chair at night to find comfort. They did a chest x-ray before starting chemo that confirmed there was nothing wrong. Please pray for the following: that Laura will have relief from the pain in her chest as we take the first week of treatments head-on, that we are able to settle in with the reality of our "new norm" and remain resilient beyond measure, and that I can lead by example and remain strong, yet be full of love, support, and compassion for the entire family.

March 14 (Laura):

Praise God that my chest and shoulder pain is about 90 percent gone! He is good! We had a sweet time at home yesterday afternoon and evening with our children and left early this morning for days four and five. We have multiple appointments today (nutritionist, speech therapist, GI doctor, etc.), along with the radiation treatment at noon. Tomorrow, my radiation appointment is early and we can head back home for the weekend. So far so good; the anti-nausea meds are working, and I am feeling ok, although already tired. Pray that this continues through the weekend. Thank you for your faithful prayers and for your love for us—we are truly blessed!

We enjoy watching our kids' sports and have seen literally hundreds of games. I am no sports fanatic, but I definitely want to be there before kickoff and I never like missing the first pitch. Week Two of my treatment scheme happened to fall during Spring Break. It didn't take long to realize that cancer doesn't really care about Spring Break or sports schedules, so we decided to spend a few days at a Phoenix hotel to be together during the kids' cherished week off of school. We had a special time with Avery, Carter, and Danica for the first part of the week. I was so sad to miss most of Kyle's high school baseball tournament in Tucson, which is about one hundred miles farther south, but we were able to get to Tucson for one of the games near the end of the week. We left Phoenix around 2:00 p.m., just after radiation treatment number eight and a follow up doctor's appointment. We walked up to the baseball field just as the first batter approached the batter's box. I was reminded that God cares about the details. He cares about mamas getting to baseball games to watch their kids play! Watching Kyle pitch is always exciting and nerve-racking for us as parents, but he somehow appears as if the stress of loaded bases and being down by a run doesn't faze him in the least. He threw well and the Eagles won.

After the game was over, Kyle's coach allowed him to leave with us so he could come back to Phoenix for the last day of treatment and spend a day at the hotel. During our time there, we were able to enjoy good family time and have fun in the pool, which we don't get to do too often in the mountains of Northern Arizona. I could not swim because of the power port that was recently put in, but I was able to enjoy the water to some degree. I was battling a lot of emotion that week and had a sense that what seemed like "normal" to me at the time was about to change drastically. Life as I knew it was quickly coming to an end. I remember sitting by myself under a large umbrella in the shade while my family was enjoying the water; Danica doing somersaults and handstands with a friend she had just met, the boys wrestling and tackling each other in an intense game of keep-away with Mark. Watching my family enjoy the pool was a gift that day, one that felt sweeter than it had in times past. I wondered silently how my family would go on without me if cancer won. I pictured each of my children without their mama. Something dark was creeping into my soul as I sat alone under that shady umbrella.

Within just a few weeks, I was officially a patient and was supposedly sick even though I still didn't have any symptoms. I now had a strange plastic device implanted under the skin near my left collarbone that would serve to inject poison into my body, in an attempt to kill some scary disease that I couldn't see. My neck was beginning to look like I had a mild sunburn, my mouth and nose were extremely dry, and everything I ate tasted salty or didn't taste at all. I knew this was only going to get worse, so I was trying to eat as much as I could to keep weight on, all the while trying to savor the last little bits of taste remaining I rinsed my mouth out throughout the day with a mixture of water, salt, and baking soda in an attempt to keep irritation and infection at bay and was now brushing my teeth with a baby toothbrush because my gums were already getting sore and blistered. Although my body was beginning to feel the effects of radiation, the week in Phoenix was a treat. We had a special time with my sweet parents and my brother and his family, who all came to spend some time with us at the hotel. A few close friends also came just to be with us. This was a picture of our happy life before cancer. A little getaway, it seemed, although we couldn't get away from what was really happening.

CHAPTER 10

Subtle Changes

When researching the side effects from radiation therapy to the head and neck, the list can be daunting. Most people have some pretty severe side effects, and they usually begin about two weeks after treatment starts. The side effects can be more severe if you are also receiving chemotherapy. The specialists had already said, "You will be getting a type of radiation therapy called external beam radiation where a beam of radiation will be directed to the cancer site from a machine. The beam (or arc of beams) passes through your body and destroys cancer cells in its path." It also, unfortunately, destroys non-cancerous cells and tissue along the way because a radiation beam is not smart enough to tell the difference.

The list of possible side effects goes something like this: You will notice changes in your mouth and throat that may include: redness in the mouth, mouth sores, mouth pain, swollen gums, gum sores, throat sores, throat pain, pain with swallowing, difficulty swallowing, inability to swallow, thickened saliva with dry mouth, changes in taste, loss of taste, swelling, earaches, tooth decay, tooth loss, stiffness in the jaw, nausea, nasal dryness, hoarseness, sensitive skin, bright red skin, burned skin, increasing fatigue, etc. Daunting. Devastating.

My "honeymoon period," as they called it, was now over, and the real work would now begin, although we were hoping and praying that this period would be prolonged as long as possible. Heading into Week Three, we noticed that the metastasized lymph nodes on my neck were significantly smaller already! We were so thankful that our powerful God had allowed the radiation to already shrink the growing lymph nodes so quickly. This gave us hope in what looked like a hopeless situation. Hope was accompanied by challenges. I was also beginning to experience some negative physical changes from the radiation.

A new sensation started that I described as a "seatbelt" tightening around my neck, and my sense of taste was different almost every day. Most foods tasted salty, and foods that were supposed to be sweet now tasted bitter. Eating was already becoming more difficult because my salivary glands were dying a slow, painful death. I began to need more and more water to eat dry foods. I was not very nauseous (thanks to the anti-nausea medications), but I was getting fatigued more and more quickly.

My fair complexion, sensitive skin, and light features probably didn't serve me well during this time. My face and neck became red and sensitive, and after the first couple of weeks of radiation, I looked like I had spent way too many hours in a tanning booth. Around Week Four, my neck became especially sensitive and actually developed blisters similar to a second-degree burn that lasted through the end of my radiation treatments. With his fire department background, Nurse Mark had the bright idea of using Silver Sulfadiazine, a cream often used with burn patients. He carefully applied the thick, white cream on my neck and covered it with gauze a couple times a day. It felt like aloe vera on a bad sunburn and felt a little better for the first few minutes. My neck eventually healed completely, with no scarring.

I was expected to drink eighty-plus ounces of water each day to help flush the chemotherapy out of my system, while also consuming at least two thousand calories and ninety grams of protein. This was to help me maintain my weight as eating became more of a challenge. By the end of this week, I had a pretty bad sore throat and food in general did not taste good. We sure take our taste buds and salivary glands for granted. It was a daily battle to keep my fluid intake up and to consume enough calories to stay healthy and to maintain my weight.

We were told from the beginning that Week Three is where most head/neck cancer patients undergoing radiation see a drastic change in their mouth and throat. Patients typically lose their ability to eat solid foods and have difficulty swallowing in general. I was terrified of this looming milestone. The thought of not being able to swallow represented a long-term problem in my mind.

March 24 (Laura):

> After a relaxing and fairly side-effect-free Spring Break with our children, we are preparing for Week Three. *Yikes* is all I have to say! We have been told over and over about the difficulties and challenges that typically follow. It appears that I am on a fairly good track with the chemotherapy in that my nausea and fatigue are both being managed well with medication. Yay! As for the radiation effects, I had a great appointment with my oncology nurse on Thursday and they were pleased with my lack of "serious" symptoms so far. Then Saturday came and so did some pretty significant mouth and throat pain as well as a new difficulty swallowing. This is expected to get worse this week, but I know God is greater still and will increase my strength (and hopefully my pain tolerance) as needed. Please pray this week that:

> • I am stronger than I think I am.

> • I can rely on the strength of My Savior when mine fails.

> • I can "get used" to the pain when I swallow, so I can keep drinking and eating as *long* as possible.

March 26 (Mark):

> We went to bed last night praying for strength as the storm hit us full force. The greatest thing about it was that we knew regardless of the size of the waves, we have

One who can calm the waters at His command. Over the weekend, Laura began to experience some mouth sores and felt like she had the worst case of strep throat possible. She now explains the swallowing process as trying to choke down razor blades, and keeping up calorie and protein intake is beginning to be a daily focus (who knew meals could be so consuming?). She wakes up dozens of times throughout the night due to the pain of swallowing. At one of our appointments yesterday, we realized she has lost five pounds in the past week, so we are stepping up our game. Another wave came when her hair began to fall out last night. We understand that this is common during chemotherapy treatments, but we were under the impression there was a decent chance she wouldn't lose her hair until the second round of chemo treatments in June/August. So the scene is now set for an emotional roller coaster, but we know that God is right in the middle of it all, holding her hand. Let us share some of the victories He has given us to balance the realities mentioned above:

- We had medication on hand for potential mouth sores so it was available over the weekend when we needed it.

- The oncologist informed us that the hair loss was a result of the radiation and not the chemo, so it should only be the base of her hairline (hope restored for round one).

- We have been able to keep the number of calories in the form of shakes, and we have a game plan to help keep her weight up (she is just mentally forcing through the pain).

- I felt the lymph nodes on her neck this morning, and they are gone! This is great news and means that healing is happening, and the treatments are putting a whooping on the cancer cells!

This morning was truly a new day dawning, and God continues to fill us with a renewed source of strength for Laura to handle this with grace and strength for His glory. It seems we often experience a "new dawn" and then a new set of even bigger waves come thundering in.

Early April (Laura):

Sometimes God gives us just enough grace for that very moment so that we have to depend on Him for *everything*. The doctors kept trying to prepare us for the days ahead, but I was only able to focus on the day at hand. I remember Mark trying to tell me what was coming or what would happen next, and I often times would tune him out (sorry, Mark). My brain was only able to handle so much at a time. But God was faithful in preparing me for each new day and for each challenge that was heading my way. Radiation to the head and neck is just not very nice. By March 30, the entire back of my throat and part of my esophagus was burned, for lack of a better term. Radiation does that to soft tissue. It basically burns the cancer cells away and doesn't know how to distinguish between cancer cells and soft, mucosal tissue. I am no longer able to eat anything solid, and it is taking a lot of work just to get shakes and protein drinks down. And then there is the whole "I can't taste it" thing. Everything tastes awful or doesn't taste at all! Once again, I realize how much I have taken for granted the simple joy of tasting my food. The nutritionist and my new nurse, Mark Wilson, want me to get two thousand calories and ninety grams of protein in daily! That is tough, even when you can eat normally!

CHAPTER 11

The "Last Supper"

Yet I am always with you; You hold me by my right hand.
You guide me with your counsel, And afterward you will take me into glory.
Whom have I in heaven but you? And earth has nothing I desire besides you.
My flesh and my heart may fail, But God is the
strength of my heart and my portion forever.
Psalm 73:23–26

Lord, I know you hear me.
You know how desperately I want to avoid the feeding tube.
Help me to swallow for just a little bit longer.

This day will be etched in my soul forever. Mark and I met my brother, Paul, at Olive Garden in Phoenix for lunch one day after my morning radiation treatment was over. I was miserable in many ways but was quietly keeping a lot of it to myself. This trial has shown me that I do that a lot. I tend to put on a happy face at times when I'm really not happy and reply with a canned "I'm fine" when things are not fine at all. Maybe it is some attempt to appear like everything is ok so that I don't have to reveal my hurts, my weaknesses, my honest fears, or my deep disappointments. God is gradually growing me in this area.

On this Olive Garden day, I knew I was fighting a losing battle with food but was trying desperately to hang on to being able to eat. I could fight through the searing pain of each swallow just a little longer. It was a struggle to find something on the menu to order that I thought I might be able to taste and that was soft enough that I might be able to get some of it down without excruciating pain. Nothing sounded appetizing in the least because I knew I wouldn't be able to taste it. The decision was made, and I ordered the soft, creamy fettuccine Alfredo, but was concerned that it still would be too difficult. I remember Paul and Mark talking and laughing throughout our meal and engaging in normal conversation. I could hear the clanking of silverware against glass plates and bowls. I watched as families enjoyed each other's company, talking and laughing as they ate. I was mostly quiet, and I was trying not to cry.

Each small bite felt like I was swallowing razor blades. What used to feel like a horrible strep throat was now unbearable. I spent thirty long minutes taking the tiniest of bites pushing through the pain and then, with tears running down my face, I finally gave up and pushed my plate away. I don't think I said much, but I knew the fight was over. It was in that moment that I knew my doctors were right. The nutritionist was right. I was not going to make it without getting the feeding tube as they had predicted. I was devastated. I was discouraged. Frustrated. Sad. Angry. I had been "warned" about this but had fought the idea all along thinking that I was strong enough to push through the pain and avoid it.

I wasn't. There is a sense of pride in being able to feed yourself, I guess, and it was my unrelenting pride that did not want to give in. I did not want to rely on some plastic tube to stay alive. I was determined that Mark would not have to force-feed me when I could no longer do it myself. But today I was surrendering. The battle of eating had consumed me and was emotionally exhausting. I raised the white flag that day and knew the battle was over.

> *I cried to the Lord with my voice,*
> *And He heard me from His holy hill.*
> *Psalm 3:4*

I prayed that I could allow Christ's strength to shine in my extreme weakness so that He would receive all the glory, but I really struggled with getting the feeding tube. I mean *really* struggled. I couldn't stand the idea of it for some reason, and I still can't stand to think about it.

Very much like the dreaded mask, the feeding tube was a necessary evil that served its purpose and helped to preserve my life. I would probably have suffered and died of malnutrition without it and without Mark's diligence in making sure my intense and demanding nutritional needs were met every day. When we were first told of all of the negative impacts of radiation to my mouth and throat, I was told that I probably would not be able to eat after Week Four and that I should try to put on as much weight as possible. After ordering a few extra cheeseburgers and eating pasta, peanut butter, and milkshakes, I was able to put on an additional five pounds before treatment started. Given my height, weight, and fairly fast metabolism at the time, however, it should have been about twenty.

It was recommended in that same visit that I have a feeding tube placed before Week Four. No way! The idea of a feeding tube disgusted me, and I wanted to avoid it at all costs. But the "Last Supper" at Olive Garden made it clear that I didn't have a choice. There was no way I would be able to eat after that day. I was scheduled for surgery on Wednesday, April 4, to have a PEG tube inserted directly into my stomach. This flexible tube would be my new means of survival and would become my lifeline for the next several months.

PEG stands for "percutaneous endoscopic gastrostomy." It even sounds gross! It is a procedure that puts a flexible, plastic tube through the abdominal wall directly into the stomach to bypass the mouth and esophagus. While I looked forward to not having the horrible pain and stress of trying to eat, I absolutely dreaded this procedure and the whole idea of having a feeding tube. After the hour-long surgery, I didn't even want to look at my stomach. The hole was (thankfully) covered in gauze. There was about four inches of rubber tubing sticking out that was secured to my skin with tape for the next several months. The Mayo dietician had gracefully educated us on how to use and care for the tube as well as what commercially prepared formulas we should use, but I was struggling. To be honest, I could hardly pay attention to the poor dietician because, in that moment, I was angry.

It was gross. I didn't want to talk about it, I didn't want to use it, and I certainly didn't want to look at it. The pain from the procedure was fairly minimal, especially when compared to what was going on in my mouth and throat. Mark became an instant medical student and reverted right back to his paramedic roots. He immediately became my personal gastroenterologist, nutritionist, pharmacist, nurse, and high-calorie-high-protein-concoction-preparing expert. He tried Carnation Instant Breakfast, Boost, Ensure, protein powders, protein smoothies, and what eventually became a staple, "the Scandi-Shake." Even now, the mere mention of a protein shake or protein powder makes me feel the need to turn and run for the bathroom. Mark seemed to almost enjoy spending countless hours calculating calories and grams of protein, measuring out medications and supplements, washing feeding syringes and supplies, making sure I had enough water intake, and writing all of it down in a feeding journal we were keeping. The tube had to be flushed with a full syringe of water to keep it from getting clogged. The ongoing care of the feeding tube gradually became more routine, but I hated all of it and couldn't wait to have it removed one day. We spent a lot of time making sure I had adequate nutrition to avoid losing any more weight. It was absolutely consuming. I was eventually able to do all of it myself, and some of the kids even gave it a try, but it was an unwelcome visitor and it was always gross.

The actual tube wasn't necessarily visible, but I always knew it was there. I worried that it could be seen through my clothes or that it might leak. It made mealtimes away from the house incredibly difficult and embarrassing. I remember sneaking my many feeding products and devices into a tiny little bathroom at Danica's gymnastic meet in Kingman. I made my way into the stall. I had to sit on the closed lid of the toilet with my knees nearly touching the metal door while balancing all kinds of syringes and containers on my lap. I didn't want to take too long and was worried that people were wondering what was happening in there. This part of the race was certainly a humbling one. I began to recognize in my own heart places of pride about the feeding tube. These vulnerable parts of me, where things were being stripped away without my permission, were often held inside. I knew if they were exposed at that moment, they might completely undo me. I had to suck it up and tough this one out.

Not being able to eat was terrible. We all know that eating is much bigger than just being able to swallow. Eating is how we interact with each other. We get together for family meals, we attend church potlucks, we share a cup of coffee with a friend, we have cake at weddings, and we share popcorn and Milk Duds in a movie (one of my favorites). Not being able to eat was a lonely place. I felt isolated and disconnected. I was there to watch everyone else eat. I was on the sidelines, unable to participate.

Mark's perspective shortly after I had the tube put in (taken from the April 10 post):

> The PEG tube has been a fantastic tool, and, for the time being, we have officially stopped the weight loss this week at fifteen pounds (I had to bump her daily calorie intake to 2600 and her protein to 120 grams). She actually gained half a pound this week, and you would have thought we had won the lottery with all our high-fiving going on outside the exam room. I often find myself trying to take the wheel only to realize it has no bearing on the direction we are moving in, which is very humbling. As much as I want to steer things in a certain direction, I am reminded that I am not in the driver's seat—God is. As a caring and loving Father, He has our every direction already mapped out (including the lessons He is teaching me on how to be a supportive passenger for Laura) and continues to give all of us the opportunity to see His hand at work daily as we submit to Him.

CHAPTER 12

"The Halfway Mark"

April 4 marked the halfway point for radiation treatments. Time for a party.

Most people thought I was *nuts*, but we planned a "Halfway Celebration" at our home on the evening of Saturday, April 6. We wanted to celebrate a milestone for us and to thank our family, friends, and prayer warriors for carrying us through the first half of this grueling race. Literally, all we did was open our front door—everything else was done for us by our huge team of support. The house had been cleaned, amazing food and desserts had been delivered, and decorations and flowers were arranged beautifully. Cards, posters, and sweet handmade signs from Danica's second grade class and gymnastics team were hung on the fireplace. I wasn't sure how many people would stop by, but we were blessed by more than a hundred friends and family members who came to celebrate with us and to encourage and spur us on through the next part of the race. We were able to connect with so many of our faithful prayer warriors who truly were helping us carry this burden. There were many others who weren't able to come who sent sweet text or CaringBridge messages. This was just one of many parties to come.

The day after the party would be the start of Week Five. We asked specifically for prayer for pain management, as my pain was increasing regularly and rapidly, and that I could meet my nutritional needs through the gross tube feedings. We also asked for prayer against discouragement, as each day seemed to get more and more difficult on all of us. I continued to look to my Savior as my source of strength and comfort, but it was getting harder and harder. I asked for prayer for my caring husband who was working around the clock to manage my medication and nutrition. I had quickly become his new full-time job!

> *Do not be anxious about anything,*
> *but in everything,*
> *by prayer and petition,*
> *with thanksgiving,*
> *present your requests to God."*
> Philippians 4:6

The party had been a nice distraction, but our eyes soon turned to the looming reality in front of us. I was trying to stay thankful and avoid being anxious, but this was beginning to feel almost impossible. The start of Week Six was a battle, although the end of these brutal radiation treatments was finally coming into view. I had now completed twenty-five radiation treatments and five of the long chemo days. I was exhausted and discouraged, and I had thought a lot about how to survive the next set of treatments. I had to get creative. I finally decided to make myself a neon green t-shirt to wear for the remainder of my radiation sessions that said "THE FINAL COUNTDOWN" on the front. I wrote the numbers one through ten on the back so I could cross each one off with a Sharpie after each treatment was completed. Anita also made me a beautiful purple countdown banner to hang up in the house. We all enjoyed taking off a number and counting the final treatment days away. I was also looking ahead to when I would be able to ring the bell.

The Mayo Clinic has a golden bell mounted on a wall just outside the radiation treatment suites that patients get to ring after completing their final treatment. The bell signifies the end of a long radiation regimen and is a moment to be celebrated, for sure. These seemingly little things helped all of us to stay focused on the radiation finish line the last two and a half weeks. The countdown shirt turned out to be a big hit with my fellow radiation buddies, so I made a few more. I have thought about designing and printing them so every patient receives one near the end of treatment, but I haven't gotten that done yet.

I especially remember my new friend Bud, an older gentleman receiving a similar course of radiation treatment to his head and neck. He and his wife were probably in their seventies and became our special friends early in our treatment regimen. We would often be scheduled at nearly the same time, so there was a period of time in which we saw each other quite frequently. Bud was absolutely thrilled to receive his very own neon green shirt, and I was delighted to see him proudly wearing it as he neared the end of his radiation schedule. He would finish his treatment regimen a week after me, but he was there to celebrate with me when I had the privilege of ringing the bell after my final treatment. What a glorious day!

Thinking about the finish line for my radiation treatments reminded me of how the last part of a race is often the most difficult. I haven't run a marathon, but I was forced against my will to run long distances as training for my high school sprints (maybe that is why I don't like running now!), and I know that the last lap was definitely the most difficult. I ran the 400 several times, and I thought I would die after about 200 yards. I needed my teammates and my coach yelling at me when they saw that look on my face or if they saw me start to slow down. Now, I needed the words of encouragement from family and friends, and even from strangers, to spur me on to cross the finish line. The end of this race just kept getting harder and further away, but our family and friends truly ran alongside us the entire way.

I was trying to pray like David did—that the Lord would make me bold with strength in my soul as I rounded the next corner in the days and weeks to come. I was feeling nowhere near bold or strong at this point. I was holding my own with nutrition, but it was an all-consuming battle, to say the least. We thought about it all day long and tried to plan for every single calorie and gram of protein. Mark had become a very detail-oriented medical and nutritional manager, and he did an amazing job keeping me on track. I don't say that lightly. I truly believe that I would have died of malnutrition if it weren't for his diligence. I just couldn't do it. It was too gross, too overwhelming, and I was in too much pain to care. It was getting increasingly more difficult to drink even water or to talk or smile, because of the pain, the burns and the blisters. As a speech/language pathologist who has specialized in the evaluation and treatment of swallowing disorders, I was very aware that I had to push through the pain and at least continue swallowing and drinking water in order to maintain the function of my swallow mechanism. I was also diligent about doing my annoying tongue and jaw exercises every day to maintain mobility.

As expected, Week Six was terribly brutal. It was a week when we really had to focus, and as Mark put it, "We paddled hard against the current to make it through the week." It seemed as though the harder we paddled, the stronger the current became. Oftentimes in these moments, however, we also felt the greatest presence of our Lord carrying us through. Sometimes I have felt His strength the most when I am at the end. And I was there. In those moments, God often put it on the heart of someone who loved us to send a card or write an encouraging note. It was during this week that I happened to pick up a little book that had been given to me earlier in the week. God directed me to a passage that read something like this:

> God wants me to discover that the grace He will provide for me is ENOUGH to endure the pain He does not remove from me. He will give me the grace I need…day by day, hour by hour, minute by minute…so I don't have to be afraid. He will provide whatever I need to stay faithful and joyful in the midst of this.

I was trying to rest in that knowledge and remind myself that even though my strength, courage, and abilities vary day by day, He is the same yesterday, today and tomorrow, and He promises to never leave us or forsake us, regardless of the battle we are facing.

I was clinging to that promise with everything I had.

April 20 (Mark; titled "Hanging Tough with Grace"):

> This week was one outlined by sheer grit and grace by
> Laura, as the burns on her neck increased dramatically
> from the radiation and the sores in her mouth and throat
> continued to make even drinking water a very difficult
> and mental battle. Laura has become very weak physically,
> but not spiritually, and that is such an incredible thing
> to see as her teammate. She continues to run this race
> with true grit and grace. We are able to make it out for
> a couple of hours (often to one of the kids' events) and
> then she needs to come home and rest. Her speech ability
> varies from day to day based on the pain, but her desire
> to spread joy is never far from her lips. We are reminded
> that even during this tough week, with God's unrelenting
> mercy being extended to each one of us, we were able to
> once again put another week behind us.

April 23 (Laura):

> As I sit here getting my last dose of chemotherapy for this
> round, and with only three more radiation treatments to
> go, I want to say *thank you* again for all of your words of
> encouragement and for your prayers this week. I actually
> had a better Monday than I typically do, and I know it
> is because of your prayers. Today is a little tougher with
> fatigue, with pain, and with the burns on my neck, but
> the medications I am being given today should help. I
> cannot wait to be finished with radiation on Friday and
> will be thrilled to be home for a few weeks in a row (just
> in time for all of our May birthdays!). Thank you again
> for your faithfulness in running alongside me in this race!

CHAPTER 13

Home Sweet Home…Sort of

My final day of radiation was a big day. We had a team of family and friends with us in Phoenix as I completed my last treatment. They sat in the waiting room while I lay under the mask for the last time. It was finally my turn to ring the big golden bell, and I am pretty sure I rang it loud and long enough for everyone in Flagstaff to hear! Several of my fellow cancer warriors shared that moment with us as I rang the bell and we celebrated with our family and friends. My new friend, Bud, and his wife wiped tears from their eyes as the loud gong sounded. He and his wife were so happy for me, and I am certain he was looking ahead to the day he would ring the bell. Bud and I were wearing our "countdown" shirts: mine with all of the numbers now crossed off, and his with just a few black numbers remaining. After some high fives and long hugs, I walked out of the radiation suite for the last time. God was so good to carry us through this grueling leg of the race, and I was more than ready to be finished with that dreaded mask.

I was also ready to be home. After seven long weeks of driving back and forth to Phoenix nearly every day, Mark and I left the heat of the desert and pulled into Flagstaff for good on the afternoon of April 26. Our beautiful San Francisco Peaks were a sight for sore eyes and now held an even deeper significance in our hearts. No more overnight trips, no more packing and re-packing bags for everyone, no more being away from our precious children. I don't think home has ever felt so good!

We had no idea we would be putting our used 2007 Saturn Outlook that we had purchased only a few months prior to such a test. We put over twenty-eight hundred miles on our poor little car in the first couple of weeks going back and forth to the Mayo Clinic and Hospital. We then began putting an average of nine hundred miles on our car per week. The trips from Flagstaff were usually made in record time, thanks to Mark (AKA: Mario Andretti). There were many days we left Flagstaff late (yes, Mark still tends to be late) and pulled into the Mayo parking lot with no more than three minutes to spare before my blood work appointment or radiation check-in time. Mark did most of the driving while I slept off the nausea and fatigue from treatments.

As the effects of treatment increased, our trips back up the hill had gone something like this: Mark would help my weak body get into the car and get me situated with a pillow or neck rest. Mark would then get in, place his coffee cup in the holder, put his seatbelt on, and pull out of the Mayo parking lot. He would look over to see if I needed anything, and I would already be asleep. I would sleep almost the entire way home. There was miraculously only one time we had to make a sudden pit stop for vomiting purposes, but that seemed to be a reaction to the new Fentanyl pain patch that was put on before leaving the hospital. It came without warning, and Mark did an excellent job of pulling over in a pinch. Our car served us well during our unending trips back and forth to the Mayo, and we were blessed by multiple gas cards from family and friends to help us fill the tank. We later had to put in a new transmission, and we went through two sets of tires, fixed multiple oil leaks, and replaced the struts, the water pump, and several other things that wore out from our many trips. But it was there when we needed it most. We didn't have any mechanical issues with the car during an entire year of driving back and forth to Phoenix. Miraculous.

Although our daily trips and appointments were behind us, we still had multiple down-and-back trips throughout the next few months for doctor appointments, blood work, and fluid/steroid infusions.

I was initially told that the two weeks following my last radiation treatment could possibly be the most difficult. Mark and I had actually marked the two weeks on a calendar. As the last treatment came into view, however, my doctor told me that it might now be four or five weeks of increasing effects. This was the same four to five weeks I had to begin "healing" and regaining strength before the second round of chemotherapy started in June. I prayed fervently that healing and restoration would begin sooner than the doctors had predicted. It didn't.

This was a discouraging time for me. I had to dig deep and really try to trust God. Mentally, I was done, and each day passed by so slowly. I soon began to realize fully that the effects of radiation are cumulative; and the damage to my mouth, throat, and esophagus only worsened over time. So did the excruciating pain. The next six to eight weeks were brutal, at best.

Getting used to being home was actually a difficult transition. I was so happy to be in my own home and to sleep every night in my own bed. My mind wanted to get back to "normal," but my body needed rest. I was in debilitating pain and was having significant difficulty even drinking water and swallowing my own saliva. I actually had to spit it out for several weeks because I just couldn't do it. That was gross. I asked everyone I knew to pray that I could maintain my swallow and keep my hydration levels where they needed to be. I eventually had to increase my pain medications again, which I really did not want to do, but even the highest dose of the Fentanyl patch wasn't enough. I spent many days with ice packs placed on my face and neck in an attempt to distract my pain receptors from the pain that was going on inside. I remember people dropping off food or coming by for a visit. The pain was so intense that I couldn't even focus on what was being said. I was embarrassed for people to see me, and I often didn't feel up to a simple conversation. We prayed fervently that the pain would begin to decrease and that healing could finally begin.

Our prayers were not answered. Waiting for pain relief is exhausting, and it can quickly rob your joy. But pain or no pain, May had come and we had birthdays to celebrate. I have always enjoyed planning fun parties for my children and was determined that this year was going to be no exception. Avery turned fourteen on May 7, and we had twelve teenagers at our house for a party. They were great! They played ping-pong, basketball, and a long game of Capture the Flag in the dark. Who knew that twelve teenage boys could go through so many pizzas and chicken wings in one sitting? To outsiders looking in, having a big birthday party for one of my children in the midst of this trying time seemed like another crazy idea, but it was very important to me. It was important to keep things as normal as possible for my kids. We have always enjoyed letting the kids have friends over and I especially love coming up with fun ideas for their parties. I had actually planned ahead for the three May birthdays (Avery on the 7th, Carter on the 20th, and Danica on the 28th) because I knew I was supposed to be back home for a while before my second round of chemo started. I also knew that I would likely be weak, sick, in pain, and on heavy-duty drugs by then. I managed to have all three parties planned out in March when I was still feeling fairly well, when the pain was manageable, and when my brain was still functioning to some degree. I truly believe it was a gift from God that I was able to plan and enjoy Avery's party, and I know many of our faithful warriors were praying specifically for my strength and for pain management on this day. God answered those prayers, and we had a great birthday celebration. Now I had to trust Him as the next two birthdays arrived. My strength and energy were failing fast.

Carter turned eleven on May 20. I knew this was the last year he would allow me to plan a crazy kid party. He had begged and pleaded for a dunk tank and had asked for nothing else. We told him that it would be his only gift if we were able to rent one for a couple of hours. We planned out the cost, who would pick it up and when, and sent out handmade invitations. What a hit! We had about fifteen kids at our house for an outside carnival-themed party, complete with carnival games, caramel apples, cotton candy, and a dunk tank.

Let me back up to the early morning hours when I woke up shaking, sweating, nauseas, having difficulty breathing, and with my heart racing. I had never had a day like this. I felt as if I were dying that morning, and I was terrified. I began to cry, and I told Mark I thought I needed to go to the emergency room. It was clear that without divine intervention I couldn't handle Carter's party. Right at that moment, that very specific intervention came in the form of a text message from Beth and Rachel asking if I needed any help with the party. Rachel is Beth's sister and another great friend I had known since her Pioneer Girl days. The party-planning, I've-got-this side of me started to reply with, "No, I'm fine. Thanks." But it didn't take long for the Lord to remind me of my weakened condition (…and convict me of my pride). I quickly realized that there would be no party if I didn't have help. Needless to say, Beth and Rachel heroically arrived at our house hours before the scheduled party time and set everything up while Mark and the boys were picking up the dunk tank. They ran the games, made cotton candy continuously, and were a lot of fun. Mark spent a lot of time in the tank as Carter's baseball buddies enjoyed dunking their coach. Each of the kids had a turn getting in the tank as well and everyone had a great time. I spent the day sitting in a red Adirondack chair wrapped in a blanket while the party went on in front of me. I couldn't do anything but watch. What was left of my blond hair was tucked under a baseball hat to protect my already burned skin from the sun.

It wasn't until later that I realized I was having symptoms of drug withdrawal after waiting too long to change my pain patch. I obviously did not die that day, and I didn't end up in the hospital. God showed His love for me that day in providing party heroes in Beth and Rachel.

Two down, just one more to go. Our little Danica turned eight on May 28, and we switched from Carter's carnival party to a cowgirl-themed party because of her love for horses. Beth and Rachel had insisted the week before that they would help with Danica's party as well. I had no choice but to accept the offer, knowing I couldn't do it. Our good friends and neighbors who have a number of beautiful horses agreed to give Danica and her friends short horseback rides during the party. One of the great things about having neighbors with horses is that your children can feed horses, pet horses, and learn about horses, but the horses stay at your neighbors'! The kids had so much fun, and we took some great photos. Each of Danica's friends received a colored bandana, and many of them wore their boots. We did a cowboy/girl dress up relay, had a huge blue boot piñata, drank root beer from bottles decorated with colored bandanas, and, of course, had cupcakes decorated with little plastic horses. Once again, I sadly spent most of Danica's party in that same red Adirondack chair covered in a blanket while the party went on.

Week Three after completing my final radiation treatment held both joy and sorrow. We so enjoyed being in our own home, and it was so nice to only drive to Phoenix for occasional appointments. We had so much fun taking Kyle's prom pictures with a group of friends and their dates, although I remember sitting in a living room recliner with ice packs on my face to survive the pain. I could barely speak, and my appearance screams "cancer" in all of those pictures. All three May birthdays were behind us and had each been special. Neither Carter nor Danica remember much about me sitting in a chair during their parties, which is a big blessing. Mother's day had also come and gone, and I was given a beautiful red futon for the front porch. The joys during this time were many, but the cumulative effects of the radiation were increasing at a steady pace, and the fatigue was intense.

We now understood that the increase in pain and effects of treatment would be more like four to six weeks. It seemed every time we asked, we were told it would be an even longer period of time for the peak of radiation effects to start tapering off. After studying the calendar, we realized this would take us right into the second phase of chemo. So much for a desperately needed "break" and my body healing and regaining strength before Phase Two of chemo. Discouraged again. I was hoping for some much-needed healing and for some pain relief. I spent most nights trying to sleep upright in a recliner again just to manage all of the drainage from the trauma in my mouth and throat. There were many times I felt as if I could hardly breathe or swallow. I was forcing myself to eat a few small bites of oatmeal, scrambled eggs, and ice cream, but I couldn't taste any of it, and it would make me gag because of all of the swelling in my throat.

Staying hydrated was almost impossible. Drinking water and swallowing my own saliva continued to be more and more difficult. If it weren't for the water being forced into me through the feeding tube, I would have been hospitalized multiple times for dehydration. The pain scale depended heavily on where I was in the pain medication cycle. There was a time when Mark had to double the pain patch milligrams in a two-week period. I seemed to be fighting a mild sinus infection, causing yet more drainage and many more nights trying to sleep in a recliner. Carter came down with pneumonia that same week.

Waiting for healing.

On May 1, Nurse Mark went back to work. All of a sudden I was without him for the first time in months. I suddenly found myself frightened and discouraged to imagine how I would spend my days without his constant care and companionship.

CHAPTER 14

Burdens Shared

But pity anyone who falls and has no one to help them up.
Ecclesiastes 4:10b

Mark has always been good at managing emergencies and this was no exception. He worked hard to develop strategic, well-thought-out plans for every problem that came along and stayed relatively calm and collected when things got intense. He was with me at every appointment, waited patiently during every radiation treatment, stayed by my side through every six-to-eight-hour chemo day (minus his favorite trips to the cafeteria), tried to make me eat until I couldn't do it anymore, and drove me thousands of miles to and from the Mayo Clinic. He became my constant companion and my personal nurse and nutritionist. We learned a different kind of intimacy as we stumbled along this race together. We learned the intimacy of pain meds, feeding tubes, drenching night sweats, and chemo pumps. Mark stayed on top of my pain medications, gently changed pain patches without tearing my skin off, and organized syringes of gross tube feedings and all of the supplements that had to be carefully dissolved since I couldn't swallow. He meticulously tracked calories and grams of protein, fed me when I couldn't do it myself, and thoughtfully treated and bandaged my burned neck. I am so thankful to God for his tender (albeit intense) care for me during this mess; I am convinced I would have died multiple times without it.

Mark finally had to go back to work after three months. He had taken care of so many details that he did not feel comfortable leaving me alone, and, quite frankly, I needed a babysitter. Anita spent the majority of those first few days with me while Mark was on duty, and I am so thankful. I was probably not very good company, and I took a lot of naps. We spent a couple of very quiet days together and watched a few good British love stories, although I'm sorry to say I think I slept through most of them. I know it was hard on her to see me in such pain and to feel so helpless at times, but she loved me selflessly and ran alongside me as only a close friend can. She washed dishes, rubbed my feet, folded and put away laundry, changed pain patches, picked up kids, drove me to Danica's gymnastic meets, and even fed me through the PEG tube at times! A friend truly loves at all times.

Allowing other people to help me with things I should have been able to do was much harder than I thought. This was a difficult, painful process, but it did get easier over time. I initially thought that I would be able to do it all, but as time went on and the effects of the radiation took their toll and pain was off the charts, I had to accept more and more help. This was one of the hardest realities for me to come to grips with. There were countless times when I couldn't be a very good mom, or even a coherent human being, for that matter, but God gave me amazing strength at the times when I needed it most. By His grace, He allowed me to be the best mom I could be during times of uncertainty, pain, and weakness. I watched God provide abounding help as my husband and children, family and friends all graciously jumped in to do the things I was unable to do. We were blessed by an army of saints that organized meal preparers, house cleaners, financial contributors, laundry folders, babysitters, and taxi drivers. We would not have survived this time in our lives without their gifts of love.

Mark and I are blessed to have both sets of parents in town who jumped in to help in different ways. My parents are prayer warriors and were worried sick about their daughter and the mother of their precious grandchildren. They could hardly bear to see me suffer, but they served as a spiritual rock for us and ministered to us in so many ways. They were such a blessing in picking up Carter and Danica for us on days we were out of town, and they prayed fervently for all of us. Mark's parents live nearly next door and were an incredible blessing to us as they lovingly cared for all four of our kids on the days we were in Phoenix. They fed them, did their laundry, played games with them and helped with homework. Carter and Danica still talk about getting to eat buttery mashed potatoes at Grandma's during that time.

Often in our society today, we see people receiving a gift of some kind and then feeling obligated to somehow repay what was given. The recent "pay it forward" phenomenon is just that. It is a philosophy to promote a more caring society by repaying kind deeds to others. There is a 1999 novel and a movie with the same name, and there is now a non-profit foundation. While the concept is good and I, too, believe that our society needs more random acts of kindness, I believe that this thinking is all wrong. A gift given is only to be received. That's it; received.

The true definition of a gift is "a thing given willingly to someone without payment; a present." There is to be absolutely no expectation that it be paid back. Our family was blessed beyond measure by gifts given during this time of great trial in our lives. I could easily fill the pages of another book with the gifts we received. This was another way that our sovereign God showed His abounding grace, love and care for us. He met our every need by rallying together the people who love us. From gas cards, meals, gifts, house cleaning, and laundry, to fundraisers and helping with birthday parties, every need we had was met through our family, friends, and church body, and by our great mountain community. Like a family that takes care of its own, our needs were met often before we even knew the need was there.

Gifts came in many different forms. I received gifts in the form of beautiful flowers, homemade cookies, bracelets, pajamas, uniquely designed lockets, gas cards for our many trips to Phoenix, gift certificates for restaurants and coffee, pedicures, all kinds of books, and a special ring with an inscription from my parents and our sweet friend Linda. Our church graciously purchased an iPad for us that we could use to skype with our children while we were away or to watch a movie during the long chemo days. I received a Kindle from my sweet aunt, uncle, and cousin on the East Coast so I could enjoy books during this time. That same aunt sent special gifts and cards to my kids throughout the year. These gifts really did help to make a very difficult time more bearable.

I was pretty well out of commission for cooking and meal planning and was unable to eat for several months. If the fatigue, pain, and other side effects weren't enough, this made the entire meal process extremely difficult. When the thought of putting anything in my mouth just about caused an anxiety attack and brought me to tears, it was hard to figure out what I would buy, prepare, and feed my family. Once again, God met us in our need for food. We were blessed by amazing meals that would arrive on a regimented schedule just at the right time. My wonderful friends Anita and Flower coordinated meal delivery on the days we came home from Phoenix. Meals magically appeared from our immediate family, close friends, neighbors, and church family. I don't remember ever wondering how I was going to feed my family. In fact, there were times we had an abundance of food. I was able to rest knowing that someone had already taken care of the details.

When you are relying on others to bring dinner, you can't be picky. You take what is given, and you are grateful. Sure, there were times when a meal arrived that wasn't necessarily the family favorite, but food was provided, and most of the time it was perfect! Some of the favorites were those that came in the strong, serving hands of the Flagstaff Fire Department. The kids always knew when the fire department was on the meal schedule and would anxiously await their arrival. When you have a house full of growing boys, those big meals are appreciated! Other all-time favorites were the homemade ribs, the stews, and the famous pizookies from our longtime friends Steve and Michelle. Wow, have we been blessed by amazing people who love us (and can cook!).

The list of gifts goes on and on, but there are a few more worth telling about. One of my sisters-in-law gave me a beautiful floral box full of verses. There was a printed label on the top that said, "God's Promises For You Today". I pulled a new one (or sometimes two or three) out every day and read it. I often times tucked one into my "chemo bag" or my purse so it would be just where I needed it that day. I stuck them on my mirror, had one by my bed, left some in the passenger side console of the car, set one by the kitchen sink, and put one in my Bible. Each week, she would deliver a new set of verses tied with a fabric ribbon. I still dip into that box of promises to remind me of who God is and what He has done. What a treasure.

I was also given the gift of blankets. Knitted blankets, hand-tied fleece blankets, fuzzy blankets. The first handmade blanket was given to me at Mark's parents' house just a week before the start of treatment. I was unaware that one of our recent black and white family photos was snatched from our house and used as a print on a beautiful purple, fleece blanket for me. After a typical Grandma Wilson meal of pot roast, mashed potatoes and gravy, corn, biscuits with jam, and a huge chocolate sheet cake for dessert, the entire Wilson family gathered in the living room to pray for me. We all held hands as various people took turns praying. I couldn't speak. Of course, all I could do was cry. When the prayer was over, the blanket was handed to me. I cried some more. This treasured blanket went with me to every single chemo day and still sits rolled up in a basket in our bedroom as a family treasure. The picture of my precious family reminded me of their love for me, and it was like having a little part of each one of them with me on those long, hard, scary days.

A dear friend from church gave me an amazing quilt she had made by hand for me. This ended up being my curl-up-for-a-movie quilt. I spent many hours in it watching every episode of *Downton Abbey*. It was hand-stitched, and the colors were beautiful. It had turquoise, yellows, dark reds, and white, and the back was covered with a super soft fabric. I still like to snuggle up for a movie in that one. Another hand-made blanket arrived in the mail the next week from a group of ladies at a local church who prayed faithfully for me, and yet another from a prayer shawl ministry at a different church. A beautiful handmade fleece blanket with tied ends kept me warm during the cold baseball evenings. I had a good selection of warm, cozy blankets to choose from for my many days spent in a recliner.

Cards, cards, and more cards! I never knew there were so many different cards for people who are sick or hurting. I probably have one of each. I received cards or letters in the mail at least three to four times a week for an entire year. I have a large box so full of cards that I cannot close the lid. I save each and every one. The last time I read through them, I counted a total of 239!

Mysterious cases of protein drinks showed up on our porch and our sweet neighbors made me soup for weeks. Friends organized fundraisers, and some people sent us money. A dear aunt and uncle gave us money and then handed us their credit card to use for gas and food on our trips out of town. We opened countless envelopes containing checks made out to us in various amounts. It was a terribly humbling experience to accept money from others, but our sovereign God knew our needs and was faithful to put it on the hearts of those who loved us at just the right time.

We were forced to graciously accept help in every form. There were multiple times I can remember a check arriving right when we were in need. Another bill would arrive, and the next envelope we opened had a check made out for almost the exact amount that was due. One day, I was handed a hundred dollar bill by a complete stranger who had heard about my cancer! We thought at one point that we would need to sell our house in order to survive the medical bills of this ordeal, but by God's amazing grace, and because of the generosity of others, we didn't. We did sell our camping trailer and our fishing boat, but we are still in our mountain home that we love.

We were also given the gift of housing. All of our nights in Phoenix were a gift, other than our week at a hotel during Spring Break. Fire Department friends gave us their condo to use for the first couple of weeks, our friends' mother gave us her lovely private guest house in Scottsdale to use for the next couple of weeks, and a cousin allowed us to use their beautiful vacation home just a few minutes away from the Mayo Clinic for the last few weeks when we needed it. What a blessing it was to have somewhere to rest and to be comfortable. God is so good!

Another gift was the gift of "chauffeuring." My parents, Mark's parents, Anita, and many others drove our kids wherever they needed to go when we were out of town or when I was too sick to drive. A good friend of the family lovingly took Avery to a couple of baseball tournaments when I was too sick to go and Mark had to stay home with me. As hard as it was to allow others to take on this job, we were confident that our children would be safe and cared for in our absence.

The ladies of Flagstaff Christian Fellowship (FCF) jumped in alongside me and picked up my women's ministry responsibilities. This is a group of ladies who seem to always be up for a challenge. It is the same group that raises tens of thousands of dollars for missions every year by selling handmade crafts, used clothing, antiques, cinnamon rolls, junk they found off the side of the road, and plants they pulled from their own gardens! They organized and ran Bible studies and planned out the annual retreat when I couldn't.

Some gifts are not as tangible. Some give the gift of their time. My brother is one of those people. He is the one who makes the long trip to visit a sick friend or travels hours to see a distant relative. He sat with us through many long appointments and was there every time things got scary.

For some reason, West Flag Little League decided to honor our family during this time of crisis by having me throw out the opening pitch for the 2013 Opening Day of Little League in April. What a blessing and an honor, but I wondered if I even had the strength to throw the ball. I was nervous. I tried practicing with Mark a couple of times at a park near the home where we were staying two nights a week in Phoenix but hardly had the energy, strength, or coordination to make a decent throw. I am not claiming to have ever had great command of a baseball, but this was pretty bad. It was a humbling experience, to say the least. You have to remember that the Wilsons play a lot of baseball, so there were some unspoken expectations here with Mama Wilson taking the mound! Opening Day came, and we pulled up to the baseball fields in West Flagstaff to find hundreds of people already wearing a blue and gold West Flag wristband with my name on it! More tears. One of my good friends who just recently finished running her own breast cancer race was dressed as a ballpark ticket agent, selling raffle tickets to raise money for us. We soon became aware that our baseball family had been busy buying and selling wristbands and donating money throughout the day. We were presented with a check at the end of the day that would help us with some of our ongoing medical expenses and travel costs.

The dreaded moment finally came where I had to take the mound, and I was a wreck! Not only was I blistered and burned, thin, weak, uncoordinated, and on huge amounts of narcotic pain medication, but there were hundreds of people watching. After a lot of thought, we had decided that Carter would wear his Mets uniform and be the catcher since he was currently in Little League. We sent in reinforcements with Kyle in his high school Eagles uniform on one side, Avery in his Thunder travel team uniform on the other, and Danica in her Lugnuts T-Ball uniform as a backup. That way, we were almost guaranteed that a Wilson would catch the ball—no matter how bad the throw was! Needless to say, my throw was, in fact, terrible, but Carter was somehow able to catch it. The crowd cheered, and some cried because they knew how special that moment was to all of us. The love our baseball family showed us on that day was indescribable. We were so blessed that day and continue to be truly blessed by their friendship and love.

Chapter 15

The Run

From Flower's eloquent and humbling post on the CaringBridge about the race:

> Laura's acceptance of God's purpose in her life, though this race is not particularly pleasant, testifies to her faith in her Father God who loves her. Laura knows that God is at work through this difficult trial, and that truth enables her to persevere and to run with endurance, despite the difficulty of doing so.

God had given me the analogy of running a race all throughout my cancer treatment. Mark and the kids bought me Nike running shoes for my birthday in February to "run the race" that was coming. Without even thinking about it, I had been taking pictures of my feet in different places along the way. Now what comes our way, but a race.

Friends and family had worked tirelessly to organize a fundraiser for us when they first heard of my cancer diagnosis in February. I don't know how they pulled off such a big event in only four months, but they did. Motivated by Hebrews 12:1, our close friends Tom and Jonette, along with one of our nephews, Michael (all runners themselves), dreamt up this citywide event so that our mountain community could show their support for us. They reserved an awesome location, found sponsors, gathered donations, organized an army of volunteers, designed a beautiful t-shirt, and set up online registration. The Run with Laura would raise money for my treatment and help pay for some of our travel costs. I'm sure it took a lot of planning, but my sovereign God had much greater plans in all of it. He knew that I wasn't strong enough to run this race alone. He knew that our family was incapable of completing this race without His strength, grace, and perfect provision. This was a grueling race without a clearly marked end, one that continued far beyond what appeared to be the finish line.

Many painful yet valuable lessons made their way into our lives along that rocky, uneven trail. Mark and I were first forced to acknowledge our neediness. When we heard of the run in our honor, we were somewhat reluctant, and to be honest, almost embarrassed. Pride reared its ugly head and attempted to convince us that a fundraiser was not necessary, that we didn't need any help. It didn't take long for us to realize that we couldn't do it on our own, and this unbelievable gift was a way our community wanted to come alongside us during this trial. It was humbling. God used the race to show us His great love for us through his people and through our great community. The Run with Laura was a great picture of God's perfect provision for us when we were helpless, and nearly lifeless. One that remains etched into the minds of many long after the memories of medals and purple shirts have faded.

Race day arrived on a slightly cloudy day in June. I had recently finished seven long weeks of daily radiation treatments to my head and neck and was done with my first round of chemo. This was a rough time for me. I had been beaten down by the daily radiation treatments, and my body was thin and frail and surviving by means of a feeding tube because I couldn't eat. I had to stay on top of my very strong pain medications just to get through a day, and even then I could scarcely swallow my own saliva. Pain was my constant companion and my nighttime visitor, nearly sucking the life out of me before morning. I wondered the night before the race if I could do it, if I could go. Was I ready for everyone to see me? To be the center of attention in such a weakened state? I doubted I would feel strong enough to go— physically or emotionally.

Saturday morning came quickly, and we went through our routine of daily pain medications and tube feedings. Nurse Mark busied himself preparing glasses of different colored liquid that would be forced into the long plastic tube taped to my stomach. This had to be done before we could leave the house because doing a tube feeding in public was to be avoided at all costs if I could help it. It took most of the day's energy just for me to get dressed, get a soft baby toothbrush in my swollen and blistered mouth, put a little makeup on, and try to swallow. My skinny, weakened body slowly made its way to the car, wrestling with emotions every step of the way. I knew I couldn't do this day in my own strength. Without divine intervention, I was going under.

Approaching the park entrance, we saw a huge, purple banner with the Run with Laura logo stretched all the way across the old stone entrance, the gorgeous San Francisco Peaks resting in the background. The parking lot was almost full already, and there were people absolutely everywhere! I grabbed my sunglasses and took a long, deep breath. I sought God in that moment in the car and asked Him to help me handle whatever came my way in the form of comments, questions, or awkward glances from others, and to give me the strength I needed to put one foot in front of the other. I prayed that He would take me out of the picture altogether and that He would get the glory for the day. Wiping away the tears that were now running down my puffy face and blistered lips, I mustered up the strength and energy I needed just to get out of the car.

As Mark and I slowly walked through the entrance with the kids, we could hear the sound of contemporary Christian music playing, the muffled voices of people talking, and children laughing. It was early morning with a light cloud cover partially hiding the intense rays of the sun. The clean mountain air smelled of ponderosa pines, and birds that were perched on the stone park entrance greeted us. We were in awe to see a large crowd already lined up at the registration table where more of our sweet friends were signing people in and handing out numbered bibs. As Mark gently guided me to a camp chair set up for me in the shade, we saw some of our friends painting lions, butterflies, and superheroes on children's faces. Others were supervising the chaos at a big yellow bounce house, and parents were gathering their children for the Kids Fun Run. There was an audible rhythm of runners on their warm-up jog. Others were stretching, pinning their numbers on, and preparing to run the 2K, the 5K, or the 10K.

Tom had asked Mark and me to say something to the crowd before the race began. Not me. I was not able to talk at this point because of the burns on my lips and in my mouth and throat. I was too afraid to speak in front of the crowd and was still getting used to the constant need of a water bottle to provide a fleeting moment of moisture that would allow me to talk and swallow. I also knew that all I would do is cry. Mark and Tom both prayed before the race began and gave all the praise and glory to our sovereign God. I was humbled and was an emotional disaster. I couldn't believe that these crowds were there for me. For us. I couldn't hide my emotions and cried nearly the entire day. By the time the race began, there were hundreds of runners gathered at the starting line. I saw so many friends that day, old and new. There were entire families and groups of people from the Fire Department. Groups from church. Groups of teenagers from Kyle's high school football team and Avery's travel baseball team. Our families were there, although my brother was sick and sadly unable to come. There were groups of therapists that I have worked with, lifelong friends, some of my clients and their families, and some people I had never met before. Some had even traveled to Flagstaff from out of state to be a part of the run. Grandparents were slowly walking the 2K, young mothers pushed babies in strollers loaded with diapers and snacks for the 5K, and little children ran their hearts out during the Fun Run. The more serious runners ran the 10K that wound around the Mt. Elden trails near our home and back to Buffalo Park.

I knew this day would be hard, but I wasn't prepared for the emotional hardship. I remember asking people to pray specifically that God would give me extra strength and energy for this big event, and He did. I looked terrible and could barely speak or smile, but I miraculously had more energy and strength than expected. Hand in hand, Mark and I and the kids walked the 2K with another two hundred people all wearing purple Run with Laura shirts. There was no running on my part, but I was able to complete the walk, which for me, on that mild summer day, was quite an accomplishment.

June 22, 2013 was an amazing day and was such a sweet testimony to the love and support we received from the entire Flagstaff community. Looking back on this day, it is easy to see how this terrible trial was truly softened by those around us. Every purple shirt there that day represented just a little bit of our burden being shared, our heavy load somehow lightened.

The run raised a significant amount of money to help us with our growing medical bills and endless trips to and from Phoenix. The event was covered the following day on the front page of our hometown paper with quotes from Mark and Tom about God's tender care for us in the midst of this messy time in our lives. A big, beautiful color photo accompanied the article displaying the San Francisco Peaks as the backdrop for a sea of purple shirts running along a dusty, dirt trail…just for me.

CHAPTER 16

Dark Days and Hair

For You formed my inward parts;
You covered me in my mother's womb.
I will praise You, for I am fearfully
And wonderfully made;
Psalm 139:13–14

About a month had passed since Mark had gone back to work. I was able to manage taking care of myself a bit better, and the kids were now out of school for the summer so they could help with bigger jobs when I wasn't up to it. I had been given very strict and detailed instructions from Nurse Mark about what medications to take and how many calories and grams of protein to consume each day. I was scheduled to start my second round of chemotherapy on Monday, June 3. I was to receive one type of chemo for an eight-hour infusion that day and then leave with a pump containing a different type of chemo. The pump was to be worn in a small black pouch belted around my waist for the next four days and then removed on Friday after driving back to Phoenix. I would have two weeks without the pump and then head down to have it put back on the third week. I never have liked the idea of a fanny pack; this was no exception. I had no choice but to rock the not-so-stylish chemo fanny pack that became my week-long friend. The chemo pump cycle would be repeated three times before completion, totaling nine weeks. I was uneasy about this phase because having chemo pumped through my veins for a solid week sounded terrible. I guess I had grown accustomed to the one-*long*-day-a-week schedule. I worried about nausea and fatigue, more "chemo brain," and, of course, the likelihood of more mouth and throat issues.

Just prior to starting this phase of chemo, I came down with shingles, which is a painful inflammation of nerves, often causing sensitive blisters or a rash around the middle of your body. It is caused by the same virus that causes chickenpox and often comes in times of stress. My body had been fighting against a deadly cancer and a powerful poison and was wiped out, so I guess I was stressed. My body was weak, and my immune system was terribly depleted. The painful blisters showed up on the right side of my stomach and reached around my waist to my spine. I suspected it was shingles as soon as I saw the first blister and called my doctor as quickly as I could. I remember discovering it at a baseball game and texting the doctor with a picture of the blister. He confirmed my self-diagnosis, and I began oral treatment immediately.

The good news was that I caught the shingles early and began treatment right away. The bad news was that my team of doctors decided I should not have my scheduled chemo while I had the shingles. They felt that it was not wise to start chemotherapy for another week so as not to cause further spreading of the blisters, which could overwhelm my already frail body and weakened system. This was a discouraging time for all of us. We had wanted so badly to stay on track for timing and scheduling and I was trying to gear myself up mentally for the upcoming nine weeks of chemotherapy. This delay felt like a major setback, and I was really upset for a few days. Mark and I were sad, frustrated, and angry because we had convinced ourselves that our schedule should stay in place just as we had planned. This didn't make any sense at the time. But before too long, we were reminded again by our sovereign God that His timing is perfect, even when we completely disagree with His plan.

We were later able to see how this extra week allowed my body a few more days to prepare for the new battle that was coming. Although I had shingles, my body was able to rest for a few more days. Mark said in his May 31 post that he could see a little change in my appearance that indicated some sign of healing. God knew that I needed another week before jumping back on the chemo path. The shingles were uncomfortable, but compared to the pain in my mouth, throat, and esophagus, they were bearable. An added bonus during this "extra" week was that I made a little bit of swallowing progress. I was able to tolerate a few very soft and very moist things by mouth and was able to get down a couple of instant breakfast drinks; I tried to thank Him for the small things and wanted to celebrate the tiniest of triumphs.

From chemo pumps and shingles to repeated bouts of thrush and various setbacks, my physical body was in pretty bad shape. But nothing was quite like the emotional despair of losing the blonde hair I have had most of my life. Other than a devastating bad haircut experience in ninth grade, my hair has been long. It is thick, heavy, and quite coarse—so thick that people have often asked if they could touch it. My sweet mom told me early on that she would buy my wig and that I should find a long, blonde one to match my hair. She knew firsthand that this was going to be hard.

A good friend who was a breast cancer survivor recommended a wig store in Phoenix. I really wanted no part in going, but I knew I had to. It was just the two of us that day. Mark was trying so hard to be supportive, and I was trying to be tough. The day was awkward, and I was a wreck inside. I had no desire to even look at a wig, let alone try one on. We walked around for about fifteen minutes and I finally found a few that were similar to my hair. Sitting in a salon chair surrounded by large mirrors wasn't exactly a pleasant experience, so I tried to make the experience funny; a coping mechanism, I guess. I tried on several wigs just for fun: a long black wig I called "El Vira" and a short mullet I referred to as "Joan Jett." We took a few silly photos and then set about the task of choosing a real wig for me to wear. We walked out with a plastic bag in hand. I didn't really want to look at it again, so I tucked it away in my closet for later.

I feel fortunate that I didn't lose all of my hair at once, although losing it slowly over such a long period of time had its own set of drawbacks. I lost the bottom half after my fourth week of radiation. You could literally draw a horizontal line around my head at the top of my ears and everything below that line down to the nape of my neck was gone. All the hair that was in the radiation field fell out all at once. And it was traumatic. Losing it was a big deal and is something that I discovered needed to be grieved just like any other loss. I learned that it is okay to be emotional and sad about this huge change. It was awful.

Mark and I were staying at a friend's condominium in Phoenix before my next chemo day and we decided to watch a movie. My head started to feel extremely itchy, so my automatic response, just like everyone else's, was to scratch. When I brought my hands away from my head, they were completely full of hair. I quickly disappeared into the bathroom to verify the inevitable in the mirror. I piled my hair into the small bathroom trash can and covered it with toilet paper and Kleenexes so I didn't have to see it again. Somehow, even though I knew this was going to happen, that first clump of hair in my hands was devastating. This painful experience took place just a few hours after the Last Supper at Olive Garden. Mark held me close as I cried myself to sleep. Tough day.

From that day on, the rest of my hair kept gradually falling out. My oncology nurses were hopeful and kept saying that I may not lose it all. To my disappointment, it just kept coming out to the point where I looked very much like a nuclear bomb survivor. I had actually posted "I still have some hair!" at one point, but a few weeks later, I realized all hope was gone, and I finally had to start wearing a wig. I remember one day asking my poor sister-in-law to cut off what was left of my almost nonexistent, remnant of a ponytail. My thick, blond hair was almost all gone. It was terribly painful, but I had to do it.

I think I may have been holding on to the idea of still having a tiny bit of hair as if it were somehow important in the scheme of things. To care so much about my hair with cancer lurking around every corner seems so vain and silly, but I just wanted one part of me to stay the same. I still struggle to see photos of myself from that period of time. I try to joke or make some weird comment as if it is going to somehow make me feel better. I wore a lot of hats, but it was obvious I didn't have much hair left. The hats didn't offer much help. I did not want to see myself bald.

In the face of a life-threatening illness like cancer, along with treatment that may be brutal, losing my hair should have seemed like a small worry. It wasn't. It was often one of the biggest fears, the most dreaded side effect, and one of the most emotionally difficult parts of the cancer journey. Not having hair was like a public announcement that screamed, "Look at me, I have cancer!" or "I am sick!"

Our hair is a big part of our appearance and has become a part of who we are. We see it every day when we look in the mirror and go to great lengths to wash, cut and style it. I vividly remember standing in front of the mirror some days, battling with myself about heading out the door. There were a lot of days when I didn't want anyone to see me. I wanted to just stay home and avoid people altogether. I wanted to hide; I hate to admit it, but sometimes even from my own family. With everything else changing in my life, it felt overwhelming at times to look in the mirror. It felt like I was looking at someone I didn't know. I wanted to be able to run in and out of the grocery store without people giving me pitiful looks and without anyone knowing I had cancer. I already felt sick, but losing my hair made me feel sicker...and ugly.

When I was around other women, sometimes their words went in one ear and out the other. Not because I didn't want to hear what they had to say, but all I could think about was their hair and how beautiful it was. I hate to admit that there were times I was envious. Even though I knew it would grow back, losing my hair was a harsh reality of the illness I was dealing with and was constantly humbling. My hair was falling out and there wasn't anything I could do about it. Unfortunately, it wasn't just my hair, but my body and physical appearance that were radically changing, making me feel exposed and vulnerable.

Our family attended one of Kyle's high school football functions just before I began wearing the wig. I clearly should have started wearing it sooner, but I didn't. Looking back now, I was probably hoping I wouldn't have to. As we walked through the big metal doors of the high school commons, I could sense that my frail appearance was suddenly drawing attention. I noticed a group of Kyle's friends and teammates who were seated together at a round table. All eyes were suddenly on me. There was no subtlety; these teenage boys that had spent so much time at our house over the years, simply were not able to hide their emotions or their wide-eyed reactions. I watched as Kyle nodded and quietly whispered something to answer their questions and concerns. I could tell the boys wanted to look away, but they couldn't. They were trying to process the drastic change in my appearance.

I started wearing the wig shortly after that devastating experience. The wig we had bought months before in preparation for this day looked absolutely terrible to me at first. When I put it on, all I could think was, "It looks like a wig!" I eventually trimmed it up myself and wore it in a ponytail most of the time so that it didn't look so much like a wig. Oddly enough, multiple people have told me they had no idea I was wearing a wig. Maybe they were lying so as not to hurt my feelings. All I know is that I was constantly aware of it, and I was worried that everyone around me was staring at my hair. I worried that the wig would move, slide off, or get pulled off when someone gave me a close hug. Wearing a wig was a weird thing for me. It consumed my thoughts. When I went on a weekend trip with friends, I worried that they would see me without my wig, so I forced myself to stay awake longer than anyone else. I left it on until I was absolutely sure they were all asleep and then discreetly slipped it off and laid it close by on the night stand. I would quietly set my alarm extra early for the next morning so that I could wake up and get into the bathroom before anyone was awake. Pretty pitiful. Pitiful, but real.

I had gone to great lengths to keep my hairless head out of the public eye, even with my cancer doctors and nurses. Call it pride, call it vanity—I call it normal. I remember discovering how it felt to have others see me without the wig when I had to remove it without warning for a scan one day. The possibility hadn't even occurred to me as I lay on the cold hard table before a PET scan. The technician came in and asked if I had metal on anywhere as the big machines were detecting it somewhere. I said no, and he disappeared. I waited for the scan to begin and the technician came in yet again. This time he said that he could see something in my hair. Then it dawned on me; I had put a tiny clip underneath the wig to help hold it in place. It had to come out and I had to unveil my nearly naked head right there in front of some strange man in a white lab coat.

As loved ones grasp for things to say to someone who is battling cancer, we often hear that losing our hair isn't that big of a deal, or we might be reminded by a well-meaning friend that it is only temporary and it will grow back. We really can't blame people for what they say during something difficult; they are often times hurting right along with us and don't know what to say. We have all been there: we wonder what we should say, we stumble over our words. A lot of times, we are unsure of what to say, so we choose to be silent. We say nothing.

Others know just what to say. One Tuesday evening, I arrived for an appointment with a longtime friend from high school who had been doing my hair for years. She always seemed to find the right words and we often laughed and cried together through the hair journey. She spent countless hours dealing with my hair that was rapidly changing. She would meet me after her normal salon hours so that she could cut what was left of my hair in private, often refusing to let me pay her for her masterful work. Sitting in a hair salon with bright lights and mirror-lined walls is intimidating even on a good hair day, but it was especially difficult during this painful time. She encouraged me through some pretty dark days and graciously cut and styled my hair as it began to grow back in. The hair that had all fallen out at once from radiation eventually decided to come in curly. The top half of my hair that had gradually fallen out was growing back in straight. On top of all of my other appearance-related issues, this proved to be an interesting hair dilemma. Another sweet friend offered to do an expensive straightening procedure on my hair so that it would all grow in the same. It worked wonders.

Losing my hair was much harder than I thought it would be. I already looked frail and sickly, and losing my hair did not help. My entire appearance had changed dramatically over the course of just a few short months. Some days, it took everything I had just to look in the mirror. Other days I would nearly scare myself when I saw my own reflection in a store window. Everything I had read said that appearance shouldn't be something I thought about too much given the bigger picture of cancer, but it was. Watching myself get skinnier, lose my hair, and look more and more sick and frail on a daily basis was an absolute battle. A battle I knew I would lose if I didn't constantly remind myself of how God created me perfectly in His image and for a purpose much larger than mine. I so desperately wanted to embrace this sudden change in my appearance in a way that would honor God, but I really had no idea how. I especially wanted to teach my sweet little girl something about real beauty. I didn't feel beautiful. She learned that losing your hair is brutally painful and that her mama did not want to be seen without her wig if she could help it. She watched my changing appearance. What bothered her most was what that change represented. She saw the frailty of life in her mom's appearance, and she was afraid.

Psalm 139 has been my absolute favorite passage of scripture for a long time, and I read it over and over. It speaks into my heart every time I read of God's perfect knowledge of each of us as individuals and his infinite knowledge of absolutely everything there is to know about us. Truly amazing! It also reminds me that He is mighty and powerful. He is everywhere with me and, He walks these difficult roads alongside me. During the painful battle of losing my hair, I really had to camp here. I read Psalm 139 over and over and tried to convince myself that I was still fearfully and wonderfully made. I knew it in my heart, but I certainly wasn't feeling it.

CHAPTER 17

Purpose in the Pain

Do I really have to do this again?
I can't do it.

June 10 (Mark):

Here we sit once again at the Mayo Clinic, awaiting our turn to head back to the "favorite" chemo room. While we are not excited about being back here, we are excited to be one day closer to being finished (final chemo is seven weeks away). This past week was a perfect gift from God in that it allowed Laura the extra days she needed to begin some notable healing in her throat as she recovered from shingles. It reminded us how He continues to work in mysterious ways, but always for His glory. No mistaking, He knew she needed one more week before jumping back on the chemo path. We will head back home tonight after a six-hour chemo infusion, followed by connection to a chemo pump for constant infusion of a second type of chemo until Friday. We will be back down on Friday to get it all disconnected and so that Laura can receive a major dose of anti-nausea meds. According to the oncology doctors, the three to four days after the pump is removed are the worst, but the fatigue will set in heavily the following week. Unfortunately, a very common side effect of this new chemo is severe mouth ulcers, so we are praying against that as we begin. This chemo pump cycle will repeat every three weeks for three rotations. Our hope is to spend time with our kiddos and let Laura rest as needed through the summer. If we have no further complications, we should have our last treatment on July 22 and then be cancer-free! Please pray that the mouth ulcers are non-existent, that the nausea and fatigue are manageable, that Laura feels strong for the Run with Laura event, and that she can enjoy the summer with the kiddos even during this trying season.

As Laura and I were talking together about these new challenges, we quickly came to a common realization: even in this current situation, we are, and continue to be, blessed beyond measure. We will continue to trust in Him, and instead of wasting time on the negative, it is much more enjoyable to spend our time counting our blessings and focusing on things that matter.

A battle with cancer is one that forced me to look into the eyes of death. It came unexpectedly and with a vengeance, without warning. I am now learning that sometimes what we think is our greatest problem can somehow turn into God's greatest opportunity to draw us closer to Him and to use us in ways we least expected. I know I discovered more of Him in the midst of this deeply painful race, and He gave me just the amount of purpose and determination I needed to trust. I also know I have more difficult races to run. It is my hope that I can run them well, simply because of who He is. Because He is enough. Because He will give me just enough grace for that hard moment. Just enough strength when I am at the end of myself.

The first chemo pump cycle of this new phase of treatment was now behind me. Wow, was I exhausted, but so far so good. Fatigue set in like a thick fog. The chemo pump that I wore all week was taken off on Friday, and I handed over the lovely fanny pack until it would be given back again the following week. By Saturday evening, I had multiple new mouth sores show up again. With my already burned lips, mouth, and throat from radiation and Phase One of chemo, I was not happy. My uvula had already disappeared-- Remember, it was literally burned off from the harsh rays of radiation. Anything I tried to eat by mouth was now going up my nose instead of down my throat because that tissue was gone. By Tuesday, the mouth and throat sores were everywhere, and I could hardly swallow again. These new open sores caused an increase in drainage because of the already damaged tissue—so much so that I spent many nights trying to sleep upright again in a living room recliner.

An added bonus to the new mouth sores was the extremely hypersensitive gag reflex, which caused frequent vomiting. Throwing up was excruciating because of the open sores in my mouth and throat. I was searching to find God's purpose in the midst of pain, but I couldn't find it anywhere. I couldn't swallow anything and couldn't handle anything in my mouth. Back to my entire calorie intake through the feeding tube. Ugh! I lost over six pounds in four days! Trying to keep hope at this point was extremely difficult. There were a lot of days I didn't think I could do it. I wanted to give up. I was weak, tired, and lifeless. I longed for the day to be over so I could take something to help me sleep. I remember then being awake during the night waiting for morning when new mercies and joy were supposed to come. It felt almost impossible to remain hopeful. I knew that tomorrow would be a new day with the potential for healing, but a lot of days, healing never came. Many days were significantly worse than the day before. So many of our friends and family were praying fervently that the mouth and throat sores from this round of chemo would be minimal, but that was not the path God had for me. Once again, my plans were not working out. I pleaded for healing, strength, and courage, and asked Him regularly for grace to continue this race I felt I was losing.

Chemo and pain often brought silence and loneliness. Sometimes a silence so loud, it was all I could hear. I spent my days praying for pain relief and for strength—literally all day. I listened to a lot of praise and worship music. I would listen to the same song over and over and pray that God would help me to trust Him like the song was saying. I knew the truth in my head, but just couldn't feel it some days. Other times I couldn't muster up the courage or the strength even to pray. It was in these times that I was comforted by Romans 8:26: "In the same way, the Spirit also helps us in our weakness, since we do not know how to pray as we should. But the Spirit himself intercedes for us with groans too deep for words." Wow. How cool is that? The Holy Spirit was praying on my behalf when I was too weak to pray as I should.

Mark and I headed to Phoenix again on Sunday evening, June 30, for another long day at the Mayo Clinic. I was scheduled for a 7:00 a.m. appointment for blood work and then would begin a full chemo day with the pump going back on at the end of the regular infusion. We asked our faithful prayer warriors to pray specifically that the horrific (that really is the word I want to use) mouth/throat/lip sores wouldn't show up like they did the last time. They were just beginning to heal from the last cycle. I was already racked with fear and anxiety as Monday was quickly approaching. I knew I only had a few weeks left of treatment and wanted to finish the race well, but my faith was wavering and my courage was fading. Somehow, I was reminded that all pain has purpose, even though we miss it most of the time. We often learn and grow during hard things; our God can do great things in and through pain. I prayed that I wouldn't miss what He was doing in the midst of it, and wondered how this time of suffering would be used for something bigger than me.

I prayed for my sweet family: the ones who might be feeling the suffering even more than me, the patient. The ones who rallied around me with my few strands of hair, blistered lips, chemo brain episodes, and scrawny, sickly body. They watched it from the outside. They were constantly fighting off memories of the wife and mama they knew and what life used to look like. They fought against the fear that would well up in their hearts as they watched my body literally wither away in front of them. They were understanding and patient as their formerly energetic mama slept at weird times during the day and could hardly hold her head up at others. They wondered about their dreams. About their future. They watched a gross brown liquid be forced into a hole in my stomach and wondered what would be left of their mama after this all was done.

This kind of suffering is never wasted and faith often grows when things get hard. That said, I knew I had to say "yes" when I was asked by a friend to speak at a local church shortly after my treatments were done. I may have committed a bit prematurely, as I was still in a pretty tough place. I was still very weak and frail and was battling a lot of challenges with my mouth, neck, and throat. God had protected me from illness for the most part while I was receiving radiation and chemotherapy treatments, but my body was now weaker than ever. The week I was scheduled to speak, my weakened immune system gave in and I came down with a terrible cold and a fever. Having a cold now is an entirely different thing than it used to be. I take a lot of precautions to avoid being exposed to the common cold and especially strep throat because it is so hard on my already fragile mouth and throat. Well, not only did I get a nasty cold, but I woke up the morning of my scheduled talk with a horrible case of pink eye! This was one of those times I began to seriously question God, and I wondered if He really knew what He was doing. I was already worried about standing in front of a room full of people and speaking. I had lost thirty pounds, looked terrible and ill, had almost no saliva, and was still not comfortable wearing a wig.

Will my weak voice last?

Will I be able to swallow?

Talk about humbling! It was extremely anxiety provoking and scary, but it was amazing to see God's perfect hand in all of it. The church was full of ladies—many of whom I had not yet met—who had prayed for me, sent me cards and gifts, made me blankets, and brought amazing meals to our family. I was there by myself, and I was an emotional wreck right from the start. Since this was a Christmas dinner event for the ladies, the men of the church were serving that night as hosts, waiters, cooks, and bus boys. The women were dressed up and the room was beautifully decorated with white lights and all things Christmas. The men served us a fancy dinner that I pretended to eat. A lot of people were looking at me and talking to me as I moved things around on my plate. They cleared our tables and delivered dessert. After the meal, coffee was served and there was a beautiful musical performance. My introduction would be coming next. Yikes!

I have always enjoyed making presentations fun and a little crazy, so I had planned to run into the room from a side door wearing a red silk robe and boxing gloves as the Rocky theme song was played. This would set the stage for my theme. Being crazy usually helps to break the ice and get everyone's attention, but now I was starting to hyperventilate.

Am I really doing this in front of all these people I don't know?

Will they get it?

Will they think I'm nuts?

I cued the music, opened the door, and ran in throwing punches. I am laughing out loud right now as I get an image of this in my head. As soon as I ran in and took off my beautiful boxer's robe, many of the waiters and servers stopped clearing tables, put down their coffee pots, and quietly lined the walls of the auditorium. Talk about scary! Now I wasn't just talking to the women, but to a whole group of men and their sons. I doubted that I could get through it and doubted that I would have anything meaningful to say, but by God's amazing grace, and in His strength, the words flowed freely. So did the tears. I remember feeling in that moment that I was not the one speaking, that all I did was open my mouth and allow God to use me to say what He wanted to say. Interestingly enough, I have absolutely no recollection of what I said when I think about it now. God showed me that night that He could inspire people through my messy, not-so-perfect words. My story offered hope.

I spoke again a few weeks later at my own church. This was in a much more casual environment at a morning coffee event we do a couple times a year. This time, I played Mandisa's "Overcomer" as I came in wearing the same red robe and gloves. I talked about being an overcomer because of Christ, not me. Somehow I was just as nervous to speak, even though this was a group of ladies that I knew well and loved deeply, but I was confident that this was a story worth telling, and I knew God would give me the strength to tell of His faithfulness again. And He did. Lots of tears, again. Even more tears this time because I think the entire room was crying with me! Some of these women had known me since I was a child. I had babysat their children. I had led ministry with them. These ladies had walked this road with me, worshipped with me, carried me with their fervent prayers, and cared for me and my family in amazing ways.

I know that the Lord will continue to be my strength again and again as I share His story and how He is continually growing me through hard things. I will never fully know God's purposes in this period of suffering. But I know that in times when I can't see the purpose, I have to trust Him even more. God is using my imperfect story in so many ways already, and I am sure this is just the beginning. He has taught me to be more dependent on Him in difficult circumstances, and I am better equipped to comfort others. He has given me a new, deep compassion for people who are suffering and is allowing me to encourage and minister to hurting people in ways I could never have done before. He is helping me understand how suffering can deepen our relationship with Him and that it is for a divine purpose. He has better equipped me to comfort others and to come alongside those on similar journeys. He has broadened my understanding of suffering and is helping me to see others' needs in a different way. I have always been a crier, but God has given me a new depth of grief for those who are weeping and has allowed me to share just a small part of their burden. He has given me a gift in being able to cry with a friend who is losing her hair or beginning chemotherapy. He is also helping me to better meet the needs of my older, long-term-care patients and is showing me a better way to come alongside them during times of intense grief or deep pain. He has chosen me to minister to others in a deeper way than I did before. God has taught me a lot over the last couple of years and He still has an awful lot of work to do in me.

CHAPTER 18

Finishing Strong

"For faith grows but by exercise in circumstance impossible."
Author Unknown

I have this quote posted on my bathroom mirror. I read it daily to remind myself that God can do amazing things in the midst of trials and that somehow my faith will grow through them. Sometimes all I can do is read the words over and over. The believing part often comes later.

I knew I was in the final stretch of this long marathon, but I really wanted to give up. I was exhausted and beat up. I literally wanted to just lie down in the middle of the racetrack and quit. But I knew I couldn't give up. I was almost there, and I had to keep fighting. Moment by moment. The chemo pump went back on, and I wore it again all week. It was removed the following Friday, and I was hit with debilitating fatigue, weakness, thrush (again), and an increase in the mouth and throat sores. I wasn't sure how much more of this I could take, to be honest.

I feel as though God has given me a fairly high pain tolerance and a bit of resiliency in hard things, but I was definitely at my threshold. It took everything I had to trust God to be my strength when I was at my weakest so that He could help me get across the finish line that I couldn't see anymore. Once again, I was weak, weary, and discouraged. I knew I had two weeks to work through these harsh side effects and begin healing again before getting the pump put on one last time. I didn't feel like I had the strength to do it, but I really had no choice.

Mid-August would bring another PET scan and an MRI. We were confident that our faithful warriors were praying with us as we trusted our Sovereign God for good news and clear scans. Somehow in the trenches of pain, suffering, and discouragement, I was looking forward to giving God all the glory for my healing and trying to trust Him that this cancer would be gone.

The mouth and throat sores continued to get worse, and higher doses of pain medications were quickly becoming routine. Then, out of nowhere, a painful infection set in on my neck near the power port site. After a trip to the emergency room and a twenty-four-hour hospital stay during which I was pumped full of IV antibiotics, I was back home, and the infection was gradually getting better. I was supposed to be in Phoenix again on Monday, so I needed to get better quickly. There were quiet times when no one was around that I collapsed in a recliner or on my bed that smelled like chemo poison. I cried. There was nothing else to do. I was empty and defeated.

It wasn't long before we arrived at the Mayo Clinic again for my 7:00 a.m. blood work appointment, my last six-hour chemo infusion, and the last cycle with the pump. We were excited to get this last one behind us. After the blood draw, we were informed that somehow my blood work showed a low white blood cell count—too low, in fact, to do my last chemo. This probably had something to do with the neck infection I had just recovered from. All I know is that I was not happy.

Who would have thought I would ever be disappointed about not getting chemo? Talk about discouraged. I was so mentally ready to start and finish my last round, and now I had to wait. My planning and scheduling were thrown off yet again. I guess I needed yet another lesson in trusting God with the details. His plans and timing are always better than ours, even when it really doesn't seem like it. We asked our family and friends to pray again. Pray that my numbers would increase that week so I could get my last round of chemo finished. Meanwhile, one of our kids came down with mono, and a week or two later, another had pneumonia. Seriously, Lord? I quit.

I was really having to work at walking by faith and not by sight. Some days I just sat alone and cried when no one was looking.

Miraculously, I didn't get mono or pneumonia. The next Monday morning came quickly and we were in the car headed for Phoenix again. This time, my blood counts skimmed in .03 above the cutoff, and I was able to start the final round of chemo. God truly cares about even the smallest details. He is good and He answers prayer! Mark and I were thrilled to be starting our final six-hour chemo day; not for the joys of chemo, obviously, but for what the last one represented. The pump would go on late in the afternoon, and we would be four days away from completing this journey. Mark noticed that I seemed a little "spunkier" these last few days, which he said did everyone some good.

I could see the finish line from here and couldn't wait to cross it! To be honest, though, I wasn't exactly sure how I would do it. I was so close, but I didn't know if I could handle another round of poison in my body. I thought about whether I could walk, stumble, hobble, or crawl my way across. I might even need someone to push me. Maybe someone to pick me up and throw me over their shoulder. I knew I had to cross it somehow.

The final lap was finished on July 29, 2013. My Savior gently took me by the hand, picked my skinny, weak and frail body up with His strong arms, and carried me when I couldn't run (or even walk) anymore. I was finally done with this grueling treatment regimen that had beaten my body down so harshly. I was thrilled that my mouth and throat might begin to heal now for good and that my weak, frail body might begin to one day regain strength. I couldn't wait to someday begin eating again, to wean off of my pain medications, to move out of the chemo fog, and for my hair to start growing. I asked for prayer for healing during this time and also for patience as I awaited new nasendoscopy results and MRI and PET scans. I was beyond scared. I was absolutely paralyzed with fear. I knew the enemy wanted to creep in and cause me to be anxious, to doubt, to worry, and to be afraid. I had to work at it, but my trust was completely in Christ for total healing and for restoration. I was weak—physically, emotionally, and spiritually—and the enemy knew it.

My entire family was worn down and ready for this race to be over. It had been a long, exhausting several months. There was a nervous excitement that penetrated our home as we waited for that day to arrive.

We all wanted good news so badly, but there were simply no guarantees. The days crept by.

Scans were scheduled for Thursday, August 15, 2013. Mark and I left Flagstaff around 6 a.m. for a long day full of scans and appointments, beginning with blood work at 8:20 a.m. My PET scan was scheduled next, followed by the MRI at 10:30 a.m. We were to meet with the hematology doctor at 1:30 p.m. and the radiation doctor for nasendoscopy at 4:00 p.m. This was a long, exhausting day. I spent each moment battling fear and anxiety like I have never done before. When thoughts from the enemy would creep in, I turned my worship music up louder and tried to recite a verse in my head. The words from Chris Tomlin's song "Whom Shall I Fear?" thankfully kept coming to mind. Just when I thought I was completely trusting God, the enemy would sneak in and craftily try to take me out:

Maybe the cancer is still there.

Maybe it has metastasized somewhere else.

What if the treatment didn't work?

Why do you even trust in a God who allowed you to get cancer in the first place?

My mind and body were trying to fend off the fear and doubt, but I could feel the physiological changes from stress building up. My heart rate was up and my entire body was tense. I was breathing faster and sweating. The scans seemed to take forever, and I was completely consumed with fear as the big white machines took pictures of my body. I prayed continually and repeatedly asked the Lord to help me to trust Him. The minutes slowly crept by, and I was completely drained and worn out by lunchtime.

Mark and I drove to a nearby restaurant before our early afternoon appointment with the hematologist, which seemed like an eternity away. We wanted to get away from the hospital and thought it might help to pass the time. We tried to talk about other things, things that weren't important, things completely unrelated to what was really happening. We talked about weather and sports. I think some people might call this denial. Whatever it was, we were doing it. After watching Mark eat lunch while I was essentially not able to eat or drink, we finally made our trip back to the Mayo Clinic in Scottsdale where we were scheduled to meet with the oncology doctor at one fifteen.

Our waiting room time was brief, but it seemed to take an eternity. We were finally escorted to an exam room to wait again. I nervously thumbed through pages of *Arizona Highways* and *People* magazine trying to pass the time.

"Your scans are all clear!" the doctor exclaimed, as soon as she appeared in the doorway.

To be honest, I don't think I heard anything else after that. The doctor may have proceeded to tell us that my blood work was completely back to normal and that all of my counts and numbers were already back to where they should be. I think I may have heard, "Congratulations, you are cancer-free!" I began to cry, and then I screamed and yelled, cried some more, hugged Mark, and hugged the doctor. When the doctor left, I literally jumped for joy! We had yet to meet with my radiation doctor at four, but I didn't seem to care about what she might have to say after hearing this news. Nothing else mattered. The meeting with my radiation oncology doctor was positive, and she gave us some numbers to which I purposely didn't pay much attention. I had tried really hard not to get hung up on numbers and percentages for this long, and I wasn't about to start now.

I vividly remember knowing at that moment that God wanted me to write this story down. It really couldn't have been much clearer had He opened the heavens and audibly said, "Laura, write this story down so I can use it."

Mark took a photo of me doing the famous Toyota "Oh-what-a-feeling" jump when we got outside. We were in awe. My beat-up and depleted body was now cancer free! As we pulled out of the Mayo Clinic parking lot after one of the most emotional days on record so far, Mark pointed out a faint rainbow in the southeastern sky. I don't know that I have ever seen a rainbow in the middle of the Arizona desert on a hot, clear summer day.

The trip home was a celebration. We spent the first thirty minutes calling and texting everyone we knew with the good news. We prayed and thanked God for his goodness and talked about what a difficult road cancer and its treatment had been. There were periods of complete silence where we were independently reflecting on the journey and what this news meant to us, to our family, to our friends. After a long two-hour drive up the hill, our beautiful San Francisco Peaks came into view. The sunshine just right.

We pulled into our driveway blasting Kool and the Gang's 70s hit "Celebration" to receive a surprise welcome by family and friends with balloons and signs, hugs and tears. We were truly blessed! This mentally exhausting day will definitely go down in the books as one of the longest and most stressful, but definitely my favorite.

I won't know why my sovereign God chose me to run this race for Him and why He chose to heal me until I am with Him in glory, but I do know that He gets *all* the glory, and we are celebrating His goodness. He is already using this race to help me encourage and come alongside others, and I continue to be in awe of God's grace and provision for us.

Healed.

I was healed from the cancer, but still present in the ravages of its treatment. I was just beginning to understand the true course this race would take.

CHAPTER 19

Time Will Tell

We knew we had a few long weeks ahead of us as we began to walk through that final valley of radiation and chemo effects. We had been prepared for this period of time as much as was possible. I was told to stay out of the "real world" as much as I could to reduce the chances of getting sick, which is pretty hard to do when you have four kids. I was beginning to feel emotionally and physically better after a couple of weeks without chemo in my body, but I had a long, long way to go. During those long, quiet days, I was reminded of all the things God had spared during this journey. My voice, my hearing, my vision, my swallow, and my teeth were all protected. My neck that was so badly burned from the intense radiation beams was now healing, and there was no visible scarring. Truly amazing.

Swallowing was still brutal, there was no significant change in my lack of salivary function, and eating was an ongoing challenge. I was not back to work or doing women's ministry yet, and I was spending a lot of time alone. I felt as if I were just surviving, moment by moment, during this time. I still wasn't sure what life was going to look like after all this was over. I wanted to feel like myself, but I definitely wasn't there yet. I was a patient, and if I survived these next few months, the future was still uncertain. It would be quite a while before I was able to get all of my calories by mouth again and maintain my weight, and I desperately needed to put some weight back on.

"Mmmmmm!"

I surprised myself one day a few weeks later as I made this noise out loud. I had a small flash of taste while sipping a mocha from a favorite coffee shop. The next flash of taste was weeks away, but this was a start, and it gave me some much-needed hope.

By September, I slowly started seeing a few of my speech/language therapy clients and doing a few women's ministry things again. I remember times when I was too weak to get off the floor after doing therapy with a child for an hour. I knew I needed to gain strength, so I began a little more exercise. I tried out a Zumba class one day a week, which was a humbling experience. I was doing a little strength training and was receiving physical therapy on my neck and shoulders for pain and muscle atrophy. I had lost most of my muscle mass in addition to body fat, and I was *weak*. I actually tore a muscle in my left shoulder one day while lifting a tiny little weight!

The power port was finally removed a few weeks later. That was intense! A nurse practitioner performed this small surgery in an exam room with Nurse Mark watching. The feeding tube was next. It was scheduled to come out a few weeks after that, and I couldn't wait to say goodbye. I would continue to have regular MRIs, PET scans, nasendoscopy, and doctor's appointments every three months for a while and then eventually every six months. More resting, waiting, and healing. During this healing period, I was given a card one day that read, "May you rest in the light of the prayer warriors, who lovingly keep you before the throne of grace." I was so grateful for the many prayer warriors who were still praying fervently on my behalf.

During this waiting and resting period, I experienced a great joy. I had known all along that when I finished my seven weeks of daily radiation treatments, I wanted to destroy the dreaded mask! Although it served me well and played a very significant part in saving my life, I hated it and never wanted to see it again. It sat in my closet for a few months before its official farewell ceremony.

Carter had an elk hunt on our beautiful San Francisco Peaks, so he and Mark had set up a great campsite with a wall tent, a full kitchen, and a big fire pit for the hunt. I decided this would be a great time to say goodbye to the mask since we would all be out in the woods. I like to call this part of the journey "mask therapy." All of the kids, including some nieces and nephews, helped paint it with bright colors. We then took turns hitting the large, white, plastic mask like a piñata as it hung from a big ponderosa pine tree. Mark and his brother David then tied it to a tall tree stump. I carefully put on ear protection, knelt down and took aim. After I fired two shots, I put the gun down and walked out to see if I had hit my target. Bull's-eye! I shot the exact spot where my cancer started (the nasopharyngeal wall) and also the spot where the cancerous lymph node formed behind it. I was thrilled to see that I hit both places with just two shots! After jumping for joy and sharing a few high fives, we tied the mask behind my car and dragged it through the dirt as we drove back to the main road.

We drove past multiple campsites, and I laughed as I watched families try to figure out what in the world was bouncing along behind my car. It must have looked a little strange because it very much resembled a person's face. Many people stopped and stared from their campsites as we dragged the mask down the rocky, dusty road. I could see it in my rearview mirror being destroyed as it bounced along.

That's just where I wanted it: in my rearview mirror.

CHAPTER 20

Extra Whipped Cream, Please

(I love the idea that whipped cream is getting its own chapter.)

With the feeding tube now gone, it was time to put weight back on, regain strength, and rebuild lost muscle. I was skinny and frail, and I looked generally unhealthy. I had lost a total of thirty pounds and was struggling to make myself eat again. The rubber tube that I loathed for so long had been successfully removed from my body, but there was a lot of work to be done. My job now was to eat as much as I could to get my body back on track. Sounds easy, right? It wasn't. Looking back now, I probably had it taken out a few weeks too early. But, at the time, I thought it was worth the risk.

Eating is such a basic and essential function that I had completely taken for granted. With the feeding tube gone, all of my nutrition now had to be by mouth, and it was a *big* challenge (physically and emotionally). Putting things in my mouth and making myself eat was exhausting. Everyone I knew was asking about it, and Nurse Mark was watching me like a hawk. My taste buds were terribly damaged and I couldn't taste much of anything. My salivary glands barely worked, and my mouth and throat were still swollen, sore, and incredibly sensitive. Even my lips and tongue were sensitive. Not only was it physically challenging to eat, but also emotionally challenging. I didn't really want to eat yet because it was just too hard. Watching everyone around me enjoy food, or even just snack on popcorn during a movie, was a battle for me. There wasn't a day that I didn't wish I could eat normally. I wanted to have that big scoop of mint chocolate chip ice cream or bite into a juicy cheeseburger, but I couldn't. The only thing I had been able to swallow for months was water and my own saliva. While on the tube feedings, I don't remember feeling hungry necessarily, but I don't really remember feeling full either. The feeding tube experience had changed my perspective on food. It would take months to gain a normal interest in eating again, despite the pain and lack of taste.

Coffee not only was one of the first things I could taste again but had also become a great friend. After forty-seven years without much caffeine, I have to admit that I have become a coffee drinker. I have avoided coffee and sodas for most of my life and have preferred juices and water. Those days are behind me now, and I attribute it to that first flash of taste back in September. Since the average twelve-ounce mocha has around three hundred calories and eight grams of fat, I began ordering mochas whenever I could (hot, iced, blended, whipped, frozen), however they could make them. I always liked answering the questions "is whole milk okay?" and "would you like whipped cream with that?" I responded to both questions with a resounding, "Yes! And can I have *extra* whipped cream, please?" Several thoughtful friends gave me gift cards for coffeehouses because they knew I was finally tasting something and enjoying coffee. They also knew I needed some calories and fat grams. I am happy to say that I am now back to my normal weight, thanks in part to coffee and whipped cream! I am also now a coffee addict.

As I sit writing today, it appears that God has protected and preserved my teeth from the damaging radiation. I still have to eat a fairly bland diet, and my lips, mouth, and throat are extremely sensitive. I also have to be careful with hot or cold foods due to extreme sensitivity in my mouth and teeth, and I still have swallowing challenges. I can no longer tolerate acidic foods of any kind, which means I have to avoid most citrus fruits, most tomato-based foods, vinegars, and spices. Dry foods and meats are difficult and can actually be a choking hazard for me. I recently shared with my family that they will have to feed me only applesauce and mashed potatoes as I get older to avoid aspiration. Amazingly, my taste buds have gradually improved, and I can now taste approximately eighty percent of my food. I think I have adjusted to the change for the most part, although a great disappointment is that I cannot taste chocolate very well, which used to be an absolute favorite of mine. I still crave it, but I am usually disappointed when I eat it. Ice cream is overbearingly cold and almost hurts my mouth, which is another terribly sad story. My salivary glands have only slightly improved, and lacking saliva is a constant battle. It is something that consumes my thoughts. Saliva helps prevent tooth decay, breaks down food in the mouth, aids in swallowing, and helps with food digestion. I used to teach this very thing to my graduate students at NAU, and now I am constantly reminded of its powerful truth. My mouth and especially my throat are without moisture most of the time, and I have to have water with me at all times for much-needed, hydrating sips. My lips are chapped, peeling, or cracking most days due to the lack of normal moisture. Who knew saliva was so important?

A recent family trip to Lake Tahoe provided yet another cruel saliva reminder. I hadn't yet ventured out on the paddleboard we had borrowed from a friend, and we were leaving the next morning for Yosemite. The boys were in their kayaks getting in one last evening of fishing, so I hopped on the board and paddled away to see if they were having any luck. I planned to be back in just a few minutes to start the BLTs we were having for dinner. I expected to see them around the next corner of the waterway, but they weren't there. I went a little farther, but they were too far ahead. Suddenly I was nearly unable to swallow and realized I had left my beloved water bottle on the dock. I desperately needed moisture to hydrate the back of my mouth and throat so I could swallow; a common occurrence, but a more severe one when I am exercising. I suppose I could have cupped my hand to moisten my mouth and throat with lake water, but I decided against it. I quickly turned around and made my way back as fast as I could. After what seemed like an hour, I slid the paddleboard in next to the dock, grabbed my beautiful green Hydro Flask, and took a small drink. Another cruel cancer reminder that my lack of saliva makes eating, talking, singing, dancing, and exercising hard.

CHAPTER 21

The Happiest Place on Earth

Magic. Wonder. Pixie dust.

I have been a fan of Disneyland since I was a little girl. I remember watching the black and white television series as a kid and marveling at the idea of Disneyland when I saw a commercial. I remember watching Walt Disney say good night as Tinker Bell flew around the room and landed in his hand—such amazing technology at the time. I couldn't wait to go to Disneyland someday! I was finally able to go with my family for the first time as a young teenager and have now been several times since. If it were up to me, I would go annually. I will never get tired of hearing "It's a Small World" play while I marvel at the uniquely dressed mechanical dolls moving and dancing. I still love the Jungle Boat ride and Tom Sawyer Island. I love running through the park to make my scheduled Fast Pass time on Space Mountain and the Matterhorn. The musty smell of the water in the Pirates of the Caribbean is one of my favorites, and I absolutely adore Mickey Mouse.

Disneyland truly is magical. I have read multiple biographies of Walt Disney and have been fascinated with the vision he had as a young man. He struggled in the animation business for years and persevered through many, many trials before his visions of Disneyland came to fruition. His dream began one day after watching his little girls play at a dirty, run down park where he noticed most parents standing around with nothing to do. He pictured and eventually designed a place where children could go with their parents and the whole family could have fun. He pictured a park that was cleaner than anywhere else and where everyone who came in was treated like a guest. I can only imagine what people thought when they heard of his dream of building lakes and rivers, rockets and railroads, spinning teacups, and flying elephants. His vision began decades earlier and construction didn't even start until 1954. Talk about perseverance! One brilliant man's vision and all of the crazy details finally came together when Disneyland opened the doors for the first time on a hot summer day in 1965. I have always thought it a shame that he wasn't able to see how his park has grown and developed into what it is today. It is truly a magical place where many people want to celebrate when something difficult comes to an end. I am definitely one of those people. When I heard I was cancer-free, without thinking, I said, "I'm going to Disneyland!"

After this kind of news, what could be more appropriate than going to the "Happiest Place on Earth?" Of course, things don't always go the way we have planned. Avery had badly broken his left ankle in the third game of his freshman football season. The bones were broken on both sides of the ankle, and the tendons and ligaments in between were hanging on by a thread. He had a long, difficult surgery to put it back together with pins and screws. He was in terrible pain for a couple of weeks, was eventually put in a cast, and used crutches or a scooter to get around. Putting miles on in a big theme park like Disneyland didn't seem like a very good idea after that. We figured we would have to postpone the trip, but after a lot of praying and planning, and prodding from Avery, we decided to go anyway. Avery had just been given the green light to put some weight on his foot by then and had been fitted for a sturdy, weight-bearing boot. He had also become a master on a knee scooter by this time.

We had a great time, and it was just what our family needed. The weather was perfect, our kids were at great ages to enjoy all of the crazy rides, and Avery did fine. His scooter actually gave us handicapped-access to most of the rides in Disneyland, so we didn't have to wait in many long lines. This turned out to be a big blessing, because I was still battling some pretty significant fatigue and weakness, so avoiding hours standing in line was a good thing at the time. We had the two-day Park Hopper pass, so we had two full days between Disneyland and California Adventure. The kids each brought some of their own money for souvenirs, multi-colored Mickey Mouse suckers, a café au lait in New Orleans, and the famous churros, of course.

We shut the park down both nights and fell into our beds happy and exhausted. Our last night in Disneyland was truly "magical" as we watched the fireworks from Main Street. We listened to Christmas carols being piped in through the speakers and watched artificial snowflakes fall. The entire magic kingdom was decorated for Christmas, and it was beautiful! I have always noticed the details, but this experience at Disneyland was definitely different. Cancer had given me a lot of time to reflect on life. I had stared death in the face for most of the past year and was now given a fresh perspective on all things living. I was now able to appreciate the little things more and see life as even more of a gift than before. This trip was no exception. I treasured the looks on my kids' faces as we soared down Grizzly Falls and waited to see who would get soaked as we rounded each corner. We had a great time racing each other around the Autopia track and laughed for hours about Kyle being stuck in a slow car. Everything had new meaning: the bright red poinsettias lining Main Street, the sparkly lights on Sleeping Beauty's castle, the detailed costumes of the characters, the light parade, and the tiny round windows we looked through at underwater bubbles on the Nemo ride. I was also able to see the distinct personalities of my children and how they enjoyed Disneyland differently: I have vivid pictures in my mind of Avery trying to outshoot Kyle with his laser gun on the Buzz Lightyear ride, and watching Carter's and Danica's faces as our log boat approached the plunging drop on Splash Mountain. Whether it was from my fatigue and weakness, or just a new appreciation of life, I was able to slow down and just watch them take in the magic of Disneyland. I enjoyed the simplicity of being together as a family in a whole new way. Although my energy was limited, it was an absolute joy to be doing normal things again. One thing is certain about cancer: it changes your perspective.

For some reason, I had my mind set on finding Mickey Mouse before our time was done. He has always been a favorite icon. After all, he was the first animated character Walt Disney had created with a friend in 1928. We had kept an eye out for him the entire time and sadly had not seen him in two days. On our last night, we finally saw him dressed in a fancy Christmas hat and scarf before he quickly ducked into a corner doorway (I guess even mice have to go to the bathroom). We sat on a bench nearby waiting for him to come out. The kids probably thought I had gone completely crazy. A pair of big, black shoes suddenly stepped out from the doorway, and Mickey Mouse was headed straight toward us. He walked right up to me and took both me and Danica by the hand and walked with us down the street. This was an emotional moment. I have a great photo that has some sort of weird, special meaning to me. I guess coming out on the other side of cancer makes even a silly walk with a mouse a really big deal.

CHAPTER 22

Still Not Out of the Woods

Yet I am always with you;
You hold me by my right hand.
You guide me with your counsel,
And afterward you will take me into glory.
Whom have I in heaven but you?
And earth has nothing I desire besides you.
My flesh and my heart may fail,
But God is the strength of my heart
And my portion forever.
Psalm 73:23–26

The previous year allowed for a slow, but miraculous healing, a lot more sports activities, another round of birthdays, and a high school graduation for Kyle, with a full-ride baseball scholarship at an Arizona junior college.

Now 2015 was just beginning. A new year. New goals. New hopes.

A little over a year had passed since the day I heard those magical words: "cancer-free." I was still gaining strength, energy, and hair, but was feeling closer to normal. I had planned a trip to Oklahoma that January to spend a week with a longtime friend who had recently been diagnosed with non-Hodgkin's lymphoma. Kristen had become like a little sister to me. I started babysitting her when she was four years old. She had a strong personality from the get-go. I remember her defiantly standing in the doorway, adorable curls shaping her face, as she refused to go to bed. I later became one of her Pioneer Girls leaders. We shopped for school clothes during her teenage years, and we have now enjoyed countless hours of conversation about all of life as adults. Kristen was in the middle of PA school and far away from family when her cancer was discovered after finding a lump in her neck similar to mine. She was to have chemotherapy on a weekly basis for several weeks and the doctors assured her that this type of cancer was completely curable. Our church family had planned for several different women to go out and spend a few days with her since her mother was not able to travel. My week was January 23–28, and I couldn't wait to take care of my sweet little sister for those five days. Boarding passes were in hand and my bags were packed. I had left extra room in my suitcase for the cards, gifts, and homemade goodies that friends and family were sending to Kristen. I was to leave from our local airport the next morning to avoid driving back and forth to Phoenix.

That afternoon (January 22), I had a slight feeling that I was about to get sick, so I secretly took my temperature.

So far so good: it was only 99.0. I was fine.

I dashed to the kitchen cupboard and took everything I could find that might help fight off whatever was about to hit me. Vitamin C, zinc, Echinacea, Zicam, you name it. After all, I was on an important mission, and I had a plane to catch in the morning.

Something was different. I remember feeling extremely sick in an instant. I took my temperature again only fifteen minutes later and it was 100.2. What! I started to feel chilly, and my whole body started shaking. I quickly covered up with a warm blanket and tried to hide my quivering body. This could not really be really happening.

I cannot get sick.

I have to get on that plane!

Kristen needs me!

Or so I thought. I knew I couldn't put her at risk by exposing her to whatever I had, but I was confident that I could fight this during the night and still make the trip. Thirty minutes passed, and my temperature had now climbed to 102.5. I don't remember ever getting sick so fast in my life!

Maybe I would be better tomorrow.

I went to bed sick, my whole body trembling. I remember telling Mark I was just really cold, but deep down I think I knew it was more than that. I woke up intensely sicker the next morning. I knew I had to make the phone call, but I couldn't bring myself to do it yet. I took my temperature again as if to make the decision for me. Through lots of tears and with a broken heart, I finally picked up my cell phone and let Kristen know I wouldn't be able to make it. We were both so sad.

Once again, my plans were not His plans.

Wrapped in a pink and white polka dot blanket, shivering and achy, I slowly came to terms with the fact that I really was sick and that, for some reason, I was not supposed to be going to Oklahoma. By late afternoon, a reddened area appeared on the right side of my neck. I had been curled up in a recliner with my head resting on the arm, so I didn't think much of it at first. I later sat up and showed Beth when she stopped by to see how I was doing. It took all I had just to lift my head up, but I managed to ask her what she thought was going on with my neck.

"Laura, you have cellulitis!"

"*What?* What is that?"

"Take a picture of your neck, send it to Dr. Tritle, and I can guarantee he will send you right to the Emergency Room."

That's just what we did, and Beth, who happened to be studying to become a nurse, was right. We followed Dr. Tritle's stern orders and met him at the entrance of the hospital thirty minutes later. Routine emergency room regimens came next: asking lots of questions, taking vitals, assigning me to a room, and doing a quick strep culture. Oh yeah, I forgot to mention that Carter and Danica had both been diagnosed with strep a few days prior. Checking me for strep was just routine. I was still convinced that I had the flu, and I felt awful. I actually asked for a mask to wear because I was concerned about getting the hospital staff sick. The red blotchy area on my neck was growing. An emergency room nurse used a Sharpie marker to delineate the borders of the area, now approximately six inches in diameter. Cellulitis was confirmed, simply meaning there was some sort of bacterial skin infection. Weird. Strep was confirmed next, but I didn't even have a sore throat.

What I didn't realize at the time was that the strep infection had quickly moved into my bloodstream. I am no doctor, but I did know that strep infections in the bloodstream can be very dangerous and can kill people. The redness on my neck was moving quickly outside of the black Sharpie border. My neck and chest soon looked like a world map with black lines drawn almost exactly around the area that was radiated a year and a half ago. This was sounding more and more serious, and I knew I wasn't going home. An IV was inserted, and I was eventually moved to a busy, noisy observation room because the hospital was completely full. That was a long night.

Bells, beeps, whistles, lights, patients coming in and out, nurses and doctors and staff talking in the hallways, constant re-assessments of my condition, and new Sharpie lines. I would really appreciate my private hospital room the next day.

Doctors, doctors, lots of doctors. Internists, skin doctors, blood doctors, ear-nose-throat doctors, infectious disease specialists. Dr. Tritle was not even on call that weekend, and yet he kept showing up at my bedside. I remember him saying he was heading downtown with his family, so he thought he would just stop by. Not many doctors do that anymore.

Tests, tests, and more tests.

I remember the next day vividly as more and more doctors made their way into my room. They would examine me, study the markings on my neck, furrow their eyebrows, and then turn to confidentially discuss their perspectives with each other. At one point, there was a total of five doctors lined up along the wall of my room, whispering to each other and studying me with intense faces. Mark told me later that Dr. Tritle said I was going to be sent to Phoenix by helicopter if the progression on my neck didn't start slowing down and if the strep infection didn't show signs of being under control within the next thirty minutes. They were worried about the possibility of my airway being compromised since the infection was in my neck. He talked to Mark about an option of opening my neck up to clear out the infection, but he was wrestling with the reality of all that could go wrong with such an intense procedure to my already damaged neck tissue. Mark recently shared Dr. Tritle's words from that dark moment. He said something like, "Her life has been saved from cancer, and now we are going to lose her to *this!*"

I had no idea. In those moments, I think I was too sick to understand what was happening. All I knew was that multiple IV antibiotics were being continually administered in the hopes of catching the infection and stopping it in its tracks. The cellulitis seemed determined to take over and proved to be quite resistive at first. I was miserable. I still felt as if I had a severe case of the flu, complete with high fever, body aches, bone pain, the chills, and now a terribly painful neck, jaw, and ear. A powerful steroid was recommended on Day Two as another aggressive attempt to get ahead of the infection. The infectious disease specialist felt that he had now identified an antibiotic that would go after the specific bacteria that was confirmed in my bloodstream. If evidence pointed to progress, I might be able to go home on this new antibiotic through a PICC line for long-term IV antibiotics.

Progress was slow, but I would eventually be discharged from the hospital a few days later, and I was beginning to feel remarkably better. My team of doctors eventually concluded that I had been exposed to the strep virus, and that due to a weak and damaged lymphatic system from repeated heavy doses of radiation, the strep caused the cellulitis in the damaged cellular tissue on the right side of my neck. It spread rapidly, beginning in the middle of my neck on the weakened side. The painful skin infection spread like wildfire upward to my jaw and ear, and midway down my chest. The strep virus then made its way into the bloodstream as the cells continued to break down. This is where it became a life-threatening infection. When I asked more about this later, most of my doctors agreed that this was some sort of fluke, although definitely related to weakened, damaged tissue in my neck. They were all convinced this was a onetime thing. I wasn't so sure.

I remained in the hospital for five days and was finally able to go home with a PICC line in place at the beginning of the week. Some of those same gift-givers who had cared for me the year prior showed up with flowers, food, magazines, and books to help pass the time on these very long days. Once again, we were surprised and amazed at how our family and friends jumped in to lift us up when things were upside down. Once back at home, I would receive regular doses of powerful IV antibiotics administered by Nurse Mark for the next two weeks. I posted this near the end of my hospital stay:

> Things are looking up this morning! All of my severe flu-like symptoms are completely gone, and I haven't had a fever for over twenty-four hours. Woohoo! The doctors and nurses have been so good to me and have been very thorough with all of these scary things that have been going on. The strep infection is still in my bloodstream, but the antibiotics finally caught up with the fast moving bacteria and appear to have stopped the aggressive progression. God is good and His mercies truly are new every morning! The swelling and crazy redness that took over my entire neck, right jaw, ear, and chest have finally started to lighten in color and are beginning to move a little toward "normal." They are taking me off of the steroids now that the panic/crisis mode seems to be behind us and there is no longer a risk of airway issues. There is discussion about me going home tomorrow with IV antibiotics through a PICC line for a couple weeks. And, yes, I told them I will not miss Kyle's first college baseball game this Friday, and if I have to go on a gurney with my IV pole, I will! Docs are saying it should be fine.

After several days of home health nurses coming and going, and Mark putting on his nurse hat one more time, we were in a comfortable routine of dealing with the picc line. I was confined to a recliner (again) to rest and regain strength. But I was struggling.

How did this crazy infection in my neck start?

Will this keep happening because my neck tissue and lymphatic system are damaged?

Why, Lord, did this happen when I was supposed to be with Kristen?

I thought she needed me!

Apparently, she didn't. Although we were both brokenhearted, God, in His perfect sovereignty, allowed for someone else to go just a few days later, and my trip was now scheduled for sometime in March. He obviously knew I was supposed to be with Kristin at a later time. We ended up having a nice week together in March when I was able to meet some of her amazing Oklahoma friends, care for her, make blueberry muffins and yummy fettuccine, and read several books while she slept. When she was awake, we enjoyed the "puppy chow" mix and peanut M&M's sent by her sweet mom, ate apples with peanut butter, and watched entire seasons of *Downton Abbey* and stupid romantic comedies.

God also allowed me to make the trip to Thatcher, Arizona, for Kyle's birthday weekend and his first junior college baseball game. After all the work to make this weekend happen, the games ended up being cancelled because of a torrential eastern Arizona desert storm. Since we had the time off, we decided to make the trip anyway to celebrate his birthday with him. We had a great time together as a family in our hotel suite and we played a lot of card games. Mark taught the kids how to play cribbage, and we enjoyed watching movies and sitting in the Jacuzzi in the desert rain. We even discovered a mountain lake in eastern Arizona on one of our last days there.

I was feeling close to normal again, and other than getting my arm tangled up in the IV PICC line on occasion, everything was good. Rescued, healed, and cared for once again. Another confirmation that I am still here for a reason and there is work to be done. God has a plan to keep using this story.

When I look back on that life-threatening experience in January, I am reminded again of God's sovereignty and His complete care for me. He brought Beth to my door at just the right moment to assess what was happening on my neck. Although He changed my plans again, He provided the urgent medical care I needed and a team of physicians and specialists to figure out how to stop the fatal infection in my bloodstream before it completely took over. And He allowed us to spend a great birthday weekend with Kyle. Once again, the angel armies surrounded our family, and I was allowed another chapter in my story.

CHAPTER 23

Words and Scars

The tongue of the wise brings healing.
Proverbs 12:18b

Words are powerful. We use them every day and often don't think much about them. Words have the amazing ability to help, encourage, and build someone up; they also have the debilitating power to hurt, discourage, and even destroy one's spirit. Some people are masters of words. Some are really good at accidentally offending someone. Others are impulsive or just don't seem to have a filter.

Most of us have had a friend say something awkward or hurtful to us. We have also probably been the one who said something to another person and immediately wanted to take it back or run and hide. Anyone with children can remember a time when their toddler blurted something out that was embarrassing or hurtful. I have a few of those memories for each of my four children. Several horrifying stories come to mind of when I have done that very thing myself. The words came out before I could stop them. Then there was the long, awkward pause. The stare. The look of regret.

People dealing with a serious illness like cancer often talk about random comments or questions that come from family, friends, and sometimes even strangers. Even well-intentioned, loving people can say things that are hurtful without intending to or without being aware. Sometimes what is meant to encourage or comfort comes out wrong and can feel like an absolute ambush. This is a very emotionally sensitive time where emotions are running high, and it can be hard for people to find the right words. Sometimes we don't know what to say so we just don't say anything. Deafening silence.

I am learning that part of how we respond to the comments of others is highly dependent on our individual styles of coping. Some of us might choose to run away and hide at times, and some might be offended, angry, or hurt. Others might respond with another hurtful comment, and some might decide to avoid people altogether.

I experienced a temptation to respond in all of those ways, at different times, but I made a conscious decision to laugh when I could. There were definitely times that I had to work through some painful emotions first, but ultimately I was able to find something to laugh at. I actually wrote a few of my favorites down over the course of the last couple of years as a tribute to the power of words. Yes, that means when it happened to me, I grabbed a sticky note from my purse or went right home and wrote it down. That in itself is funny to me. I still laugh out loud now as I read these comments and questions.

Most people I knew were aware of the eating challenges I was facing, and they were terribly worried. Everyone wanted me to be able to eat normally again and to be able to taste the foods that I loved. It seemed to be a big deal to many. That said, I had an ongoing dialogue with people about food, swallowing, saliva, salivary glands, and taste buds. It is no surprise, then, that I was asked the following questions almost continually: "Can you taste that?" "Can you taste *that*?" and, "How about that?"

With my outward appearance always changing and the drastic weight loss I was experiencing, friends and strangers were also very concerned about my significant weight loss and skinny frame. They just couldn't help themselves from saying things like: "Your face looks different", "Have you gained any weight yet?" "You need to eat more!", or "You are so f####### skinny!"

Some other favorites are:

"Is your hair starting to grow back yet?"

"Can you even talk?"

"Do you have any saliva yet?"

"Do you still have that feeding tube thing?"

"Are you able to eat yet?"

"How is that *thing* on your head?" (Eyes were looking at the top of my head, with a quick gesture in the direction of my wig).

"I haven't seen you in a while. John was right—you *are* skinny and wearing a wig!" (name changed, of course, to protect the perpetrator).

Just recently at a church function, someone I hadn't seen for a few months literally reached over and tugged on my hair and asked, "Is that your real hair?" I have thought about this one many times because if I were, in fact, still wearing a wig, she would have had it in her hand.

There were, of course, times of awkward conversation with people, often times at church or in a grocery store— nowhere to run, nowhere to hide. The evening I was scheduled to speak at a church about my cancer for the first time was preceded by a brief, painful conversation. I would be standing in front of two hundred people in a couple of hours, and I was already very conscious of my appearance. I was recently cancer-free, but I was significantly underweight, I was wearing a wig, and still looked quite sickly. It had taken me a long time to figure out what I could wear that wouldn't exacerbate any or all of those things. After changing my clothes about five times, I had finally settled on a cream-colored shirt and black pants with tall boots and a light pink jacket. The outfit was okay; it was the shell of a body underneath that was concerning.

"You look *awfully* thin, Laura...how are you?"

I nervously and graciously replied saying, "I am actually recently cancer-free and am now trying to gain some of my strength back."

The stares came in with a furrowed brow and intense eyes. The speech slowed. "Because you really do look *awfully* thin!"

I tried to smile and responded as graciously as I could while fighting back the tears that I knew were on their way: "I know. I am pretty skinny, and I need to gain some weight back, but I'm slowly getting there."

And then, the words came just one more time: "I mean, are you *really* okay? Because you are *awfully* thin!" I forced a quick smile and exited stage left to the bathroom to cry.

Words can hurt and often leave scars, but choosing to laugh at some of my most painful comments or questions has been a good strategy for me. There are other kinds of scars that can't be laughed away. I try to see them as reminders of what God has done to heal me.

Scars are a natural part of our body's healing process. They are a result of the body working to repair some kind of wound in the skin or other tissue underneath. Most significant wounds result in some degree of scarring, although they often fade or change color and shape with time. Scars are actually pretty amazing if you think about them. After doing some research I found out that they are made of the same protein as the wounded tissue, but how a scar is put together is altogether different. They do not contain sweat glands or hair follicles, and their sensitivity is often lessened. Avery has a terrible scar on his ankle from his ankle surgery that he has absolutely no feeling in. Sometimes a scar can cause decreased muscle function, like the scar tissue I now have in my neck from radiation.

Most of us have scars of some kind: Scars on our knees from falling as a small child, scars from surgeries, scars from cutting ourselves while cooking, or scars from running into things. Some of us have emotional scars from painful experiences or trauma. A lot of people try to hide their scars or pretend they don't exist because they are ugly or they can be reminders of deep, emotional pain. Others might be reminded of a traumatic event when they look at their scar. Scars often remind me of the past.

I have multiple small scars from being an active, sometimes clumsy kid. I mentioned earlier my encounter with a piano bench in Alaska, and I also fell off of my brother's shoulders onto an ice rink. In the second grade, I was pushed off of an eighteen-foot slide during one of my brother's little league games and met the pavement with my face. I was bitten by a scary St. Bernard as I was walking our dog through a neighborhood in sixth grade, and I had an appendectomy and a breast lumpectomy both in my last year of high school. I now have some additional battle wounds from cancer and the treatment that God used to save my life. The right side of my neck carries a scar where Dr. Tritle removed the lymph node for a biopsy and first discovered I had cancer. Just below my left clavicle is a scar where the power port rested for the better part of a year to deliver powerful yet poisonous chemotherapy drugs, various medications, and IV fluids when I needed them. Just above the clavicle on the same side is a scar from the insertion point of the tubing that was fed from the power port into one of the large central veins whose job was to deliver blood to my heart. This was a very vascular wound that was not able to heal until the poisons of chemotherapy were completely out of my body, after all of the treatments were over. There was a long period of time when I thought it would never heal, but it finally did.

The feeding tube was removed on September 12, 2013. I wanted that terrible thing out as soon as possible! This was a simple procedure for which I was awake, and the doctor simply pulled it out through the existing hole that was already in my stomach. Gross! I was then literally left with a hole in my stomach that the doctors said would close on its own within a few days. I was highly skeptical that this hole leading directly into my stomach would heal on its own. In fact, several people had shared horror stories with me about the hole not healing completely, leaking stomach contents, smelling terribly, and making awful bodily function noises. Yikes! I was completely grossed out and scared to death of what was going to happen. I distinctly remember the day the tube was finally removed. Several hours after the surgery, I finally was brave enough to pull the gauze bandage back. I somehow wanted to see the hole that would be left in my stomach. I think my eyes may have been closed as I slowly and cautiously began to pull the tape from my sensitive skin. When I eventually opened my eyes, I was shocked to see that the hole had already closed! I am still amazed at how quickly that happened and how unbelievable and miraculous the human body is. The scar left on my stomach now looks like I have been shot point-blank with a handgun.

There are days that my scars stand out to me when I look in the mirror. Some days I notice them more than others. Though they have faded slightly and I have gotten somewhat used to them, their presence is always there. Sometimes I feel that they are simply there to humble me and to remind me. They are now part of me and serve as a small reminder of the amazing, miraculous healing that God alone has given me. I might initially see them as ugly, but God quickly reminds me that those scars represent healing. My scars represent life. As the song "Great Things" by Elevation Worship says, "I am thankful for the scars I bear. They declare that He is my healer."

CHAPTER 24

Here Again?

October 19, 2015.

Two years is a long time. Two years had passed since I heard those beautiful, perfect words, "You are cancer-free." I have graduated along a progression from going down to the Mayo Clinic every three months to every six months. It was that uneasy time again, and I had my full day of tests and scans on the big dry erase calendar in the kitchen for months. This was routine, and I had been here many times. As it usually does, however, anxiety and fear snuck up on me and worked their way into my soul as the date written with black ink drew closer.

I went alone that day. Mark had been with me for all of these long days of tests and scans, but he had a work commitment that he was not able to get out of this time. My dad was already in the Phoenix area with my brother, Paul, to help him on a house project, so they were going to be with me for part of the day, and we planned on eating lunch together. This day was different, but completely fine. I had done this so many times now that I knew exactly what to expect: sitting, waiting, worrying, sitting some more, lying still in big white machines, praying that I can swallow without my water bottle close by, waiting some more, having scopes up my nose and down my throat, then finally, hearing some valued words from the doctor as she reviews the scans from the morning. Routine.

As I walked into the Mayo clinic this particular morning, I saw the sign with big white letters that says, "NUCLEAR MEDICINE CHECK-IN." This always sounds a little scary to me and I often wonder about the harm on my body each time radioactive material was pumped into my veins. I walked past several long rows of matching chairs in the waiting room where moms, dads, grandparents, and friends waited for their name or the name of a loved one to be called. People were here for different reasons. Regular checkups, heart issues, tests and scans, GI problems, cancer. Some appeared to be calm and relaxed, some were wrestling with worry and fear. Many were sick, yellow in color, and weak. I walked down the hall to the desk where I was greeted by a young woman in her mid-twenties. She escorted me to the dressing room where I was handed a clean gown, white scrub pants, and protective booties.

I found my seat in a smaller waiting room while I waited for my name to be called. Across from me sat an older man, probably in his eighties, talking to his friend, similar in age, about heart surgery and stints. A white-haired woman with a walker was to his left. We were all wearing matching blue or pink gowns with meaningless patterns and white pants. Technicians periodically walked in and out of the room with their white lab coats, rubber gloves, and blue plastic booties. The room was quiet other than the faint sound of an HGTV home improvement show running in the corner.. White plastic bags with the words "PERSONAL BELONGINGS" written in big letters laid scattered around the room that day because there were no lockers available. After about ten minutes, my name was called to have the IV placed in my arm. My veins cooperated again, so I quickly returned to my seat minutes later with my IV in place. After another brief wait and another personal escort, I was now seated in an olive green recliner in my "private suite" as radioactive material began traveling throughout my body to be absorbed by my vital organs and tissues, looking for places to light up. Looking for cancer, in a sense. The room was cold. The recliner, an extra IV pole, boxes of blue rubber gloves, a small trash can, and a wall-mounted hand sanitizer dispenser were my only companions for the next hour. Fortunately, I was able to bring my water bottle, a journal, and my phone for music. The most treasured part of this period of solitary confinement was the beloved warm blanket.

"Two, please."

I could hear a technician outside the door explaining how nuclear medicine works to someone who had never had a PET scan. I heard the big, white, sterile machine measuring out someone else's radioactive dose. The thought of a radioactive tracer looking for disease is a little disturbing, but the PET scan process would translate to a beautiful, three-dimensional color picture of my body from head to toe. The glucose-based tracer goes to places in the body that use glucose for energy (I Googled this earlier so I would understand what was happening). Apparently, cancerous tissue uses glucose differently than healthy tissue, so cancer will literally light up on a PET scan. I remember having prayed for a complete "blackout" in the past. The PET scan can detect cancer, show the stages of cancer, show the spread of cancer, and show how well a treatment is working—or not working. I was, of course, hoping that it would show absolutely *nothing*. Lights out.

All I could hear was the quiet. I was alone in this stark room. Alone with my thoughts. Alone with God. I prayed for peace and for clear scans with no sign of cancer creeping back into my body. I prayed that I would have saliva during the scan. (It seems so silly, but an hour in a machine without saliva and without my water bottle can seem like an eternity!) The hour in isolation went by so slowly. I tried to pray, but all I could think about was what I was going to eat as soon as I was finished. I hadn't eaten anything since dinner the night before, and I am definitely someone who needs a little protein in the morning—and now coffee! Quiet.

I wrote my thoughts and prayers in a journal. I heard my stomach growling. I hit play on a Chris Tomlin song on my iPhone to drown out the sounds of hunger and to distract me from the silence. The long hour came to an end and the heavy, dark wooden door slowly opened. A dark-haired woman in a lab coat stood on the other side to guide me down the hall. Another cold, all-white room: white floors, white lab coats, white walls, white ceilings, white machines. Just white. The test itself went by rather quickly and I was given a "BELONGINGS" bag so I could change.

My dad and Paul met me in the lobby after the PET scan, and we went to Pei Wei for a quick lunch before my MRI that was scheduled for noon. We talked and laughed as we enjoyed our noodles and sesame chicken. Time spent with my dad and brother is always entertaining. We then drove Paul's car back to the Mayo Clinic when we were done. We sat in the waiting room for about ten minutes before my name was called. I would be busy now for another couple of hours and then more appointments with nurses and doctors. We had decided it made the most sense for them to head to Paul's house so they could spend the afternoon on his backyard project. I would be fine. I was soon guided to yet another dressing room. Another pair of white pants, a pink gown, and blue plastic booties. More HGTV on in the waiting room. I had a headache now, and I was nervous about the MRI. It always takes a long time, is very loud, and is fairly anxiety-provoking with the head and face "lockdown," as I call it. I was worried about my dry mouth and throat during the long test. I was worried about the results.

This was where the enemy liked to creep in and pull the rug out from under me. He whispered doubt into my already vulnerable ear. He told me the cancer had probably come back or had gone somewhere else; he told me I wouldn't be able to swallow during the test; he reminded me of my fears about the stressful procedure that was to come; he told me I was alone. With a headache already and fear taking up residence in my heart, I was in a bad place. More waiting.

"Laura Wilson?" I took a deep breath and followed the technician down the hall.

"OK, we're going to go ahead and get started. Go ahead and lie down."

I was handed small rubber earplugs that I quickly put into place. Cotton padding was placed between my ears and the edges of the headrest to dampen some of the noise from the machine. My body was strapped down, I was covered with a treasured warm blanket, and I was handed a small, squishy emergency call light in case I needed out. Somehow this squishy ball was supposed to make me feel safe and in control. I wasn't so sure. Without warning, the white, heavy plastic box was locked around my face to keep me from moving. I felt my heart rate increase and my breathing went into panic mode. The next piece of the machine was then attached on top of the first and a voice said, "Doing ok?"

Not really, actually. But I said nothing.

I thought to myself, "I have done this many times before. It's ok. Try to relax." I asked the Lord to give me a distraction. Give me a song. Nothing. I felt panic settling in and needed just a minute to breathe, but the machine began pulling my body into the white tube where I would remain motionless for the next hour and a half.

I closed my eyes so that I didn't see how close the casket-like tube was to my face. A stranger's muffled voice was piped into a small speaker that said, "This first series will be about six minutes," and the deafening sounds of the MRI machine began immediately. All I could hear was what sounded like a jackhammer all around my head. I had nothing to distract me. No song to sing. All I had was fear. I tried to pray. I tried to think of any worship song I could think of. Nothing. I tried to count the minutes and start a running countdown in my mind. If this series was six minutes, then I would only have about another hour and twenty minutes after this. This strategy was definitely not helping. My already dry mouth and throat were getting drier. Every muscle in my body was tight. My headache was getting more intense with every beat of the machine. I contemplated squeezing the "I need out" ball, but I knew that I would have to start the whole process over. I was helpless and scared. I tried to convince myself that I could do this, that I wasn't going to die in the MRI machine.

"Lord, give me peace and calm. Help me to breathe. Slow my heart rate down. I know you are in control. Give me a song to sing. Please help me, I can't think of any songs!" Still nothing.

"The next series will be twelve minutes."

Twelve minutes! Breathe!

I tried to keep my eyes closed, but instinctively they kept opening. All I could see was white. I saw the heavy plastic box locked around my face and head. I felt my heart rate increase, and I could almost hear the pounding in my chest. I could see the inside of the MRI machine, about eight inches away from my face. I could feel the inside of the large tube pressing in on my shoulders and hips. My neck ached, my shoulders began to hurt, and my arms were falling asleep. I recognized that I was allowing fear to take over, but I couldn't seem to relax. I was finally able to pray, and in that moment, God gave me a visual list of people to pray for. I prayed for everyone on the list and then anyone else I could think of. I prayed for my husband, for my kids, my family and friends. I prayed for our church, and I visually pictured each lady in my Tuesday morning Bible study and prayed for her specifically.

"This next series will be six minutes."

I figured I should be almost done. I made the mistake of asking the technician if we were almost done, and she promptly said, "Oh no, we still have about forty minutes left."

I battled fear, anxiety, and full-on panic for the next forty minutes. For some reason, the MRI lasted over an hour and a half this time. The muffled voices finally stopped talking to me, and my body was slowly moved out of the machine. I spoke with the technicians about my increasing fear after I was finally off of the table. They shared with me that some people who have repeated MRIs of the head and neck tend to struggle more with each one. I decided that I was now in that category. They proceeded to tell me that those patients usually take some sort of medication to help them relax. Sign me up! I might actually consider it for the next one. I already have anxiety about it if I stop and think too much.

I was walked back down a long white hall to a dressing room to get out of my "beautiful" hospital gown. I smiled at the technician and said thank you. As I closed the door behind me, I was overwhelmed with the stress and fear that I had been battling for the last few hours. My emotions completely took over, and I began to cry. It all came crashing down on me in that moment. Everything I had been fighting and holding inside came flooding out. I wept in that dressing room for about five minutes. Then I got dressed and walked down the silent hall toward the waiting room.

Now I could breathe and I was on a mission: find a Starbucks for some much-needed caffeine and a treat! After just a few minutes of driving, I found a Starbucks in the same shopping center as Hobby Lobby. How lucky can a girl get? I was looking for a specific tray for our coffee table that I had seen months before when I was in Oklahoma with Kristen. It had been recently marked down to 50 percent off. It went immediately into my cart. I had about an hour to spare before heading back to meet with my nurse and the radiation oncology doctor for nasendoscopy and my results. Although it is not exactly a pleasant experience to have a flexible scope guided up my nose and down my throat, I knew that part should be easy compared to the long MRI. I walked up and down the aisles of Hobby Lobby admiring all things cute and crafty and felt like I needed to redecorate my entire house. This was a mindless distraction. I was purposely occupying my thoughts with meaningless things, but underneath it all, was doubt and worry. I knew in my heart that bad news was coming.

I was back at the Mayo Clinic by three thirty for my three forty-five appointment with my nurse. Waiting, waiting, and more waiting. After a checkup and more questions, the nurse said she thought everything was fine, but the doctor needed to talk to me.

Talk to me?

About what?

My emotionally exhausted, doubting mind was sure there was something wrong. I tried to keep my emotions tucked away as the doctor had come in for the next procedure. Nasendoscopy. My favorite. Epinephrine followed by numbing solution was squirted up my already sensitive nose. A long, flexible tube with a light and a camera on the end were then fed up my right nostril and down my throat. The doctor moved the light around, looking for anything abnormal. Looking for cancer. Finally, a few long vowel sounds as she watched my vocal folds in action and I was done.

"Everything looks good. Your scans are all normal and there is nothing that looks different or concerning."

"*What?* All that fear and debilitating anxiety and worry, and everything is fine?"

Relief washed over me. My fears were wiped away in an instant, and I was so grateful. Exhausted and drained, but grateful. The doctor asked a few more questions and followed up with my ongoing mouth and throat issues. She mentioned again that I could try acupuncture for a slim chance that it might help improve salivary function. I keep forgetting to do that. It may have something to do with the idea of lots of little needles in my face, but I'm not sure. I asked about the recurrence of my cancer, assuming that two years of remission was a big deal. It was a big deal, but the doctor said she wanted to see another year "under my belt" before we could all rest a bit more. I decided a long time ago not to look at numbers, percentages, or likelihoods. I plan to try to trust God with the next year and pray that it goes by quickly, but a year is a long time to ignore the long, dark shadows of cancer.

CHAPTER 25

Hope Beyond Suffering

Today you have hope, not because people like
you or because situations are easy,
but because God has placed his unshakable love on you.
Paul Tripp

December 29, 2013 (Laura):

This year has been one marked by a long, difficult race
God called me to run starting in January. I crossed the
finish line of treatment in August (by God's amazing,
abounding grace) and had a clear PET scan and MRI
at that time, Praise God! I have since had another set of
updated scans (mid-December) and everything is still
clear! All of my blood work and numbers are normal or
above normal! My energy level and strength continue
to improve on a weekly basis, and I am trusting Him to
restore my body completely.

I am a cancer survivor, but cancer does not define me.
I am defined by my Savior. I am healed.
Although I believed all along that my God was bigger than the worst
of cancers and that He was more than able to heal, there was no certainty
of that outcome. He could have terminated my time on earth and left my

husband a widower and my children without their mama. I am not exactly sure why, but He has chosen to spare me for now.

I often wonder if I would still be able to say that God is good if I weren't healed and I knew cancer was going to take my life, or if I were terribly disfigured from surgery or treatment. Would I still have faith in Him if life after cancer was miserable?

I wasn't sure how this story was going to turn out or what life would be like when treatment was over. I wasn't confident that the cancer would be gone, or that the treatment would even work. I wondered what terrible side effects from radiation would be lifelong. I worried about the future constantly. But somehow throughout this arduous race, I was reminded again and again that our God is a God who cares about our suffering, and He cares about the details of our lives. He only allows things to come into our lives that will ultimately be for His glory and our good. I didn't exactly know what that meant, but I had to trust in that.

I believed it in my head, but did I really believe it in my heart? This was another hard reality I had to wrestle with. In fact, three years later, I still need constant reminding that it is possible to give God the glory, even to be thankful, when life hurts. It was so incredibly hard to see this truth in the midst of uncertainty, pain and suffering, but there were times He gave me a little glimpse of His sovereign hand at work along the way. I need these little reminders. He continues to give me glimpses of the many, many ways He is using my story for His purposes. He is requiring me to constantly share it with others and He keeps asking me to trust Him while I wait for results after repeated medical tests. He is still asking me to trust Him with my questions and with some of the physical challenges left in radiation's wake.

The hardest parts of this race are behind me now, and I would be lying if I didn't admit that I am glad the race is over. The treatments that God used to save my life nearly killed me. Thankfully, new techniques are being developed every day to decrease the brutal side effects of radiation to the head and neck. The Mayo Clinic in Scottsdale has already opened a new building which houses a brand new type of radiation technology. Radiation beams can now be directed even more specifically at their target, decreasing some of the harsh side effects. That gives me hope.

I also find hope in how my body continues to heal. My overall strength and energy have essentially been restored, but there are many residual challenges. I am no longer praying that I can swallow, but swallowing is still not perfect. Most of my salivary glands were brutally murdered by radiation, so I have come to grips with the fact that my mouth and throat issues will probably be lifelong battles. That means that I really will be surviving on mashed potatoes and applesauce when I am old. For now, I have to think carefully about what I eat. I even have to think about when I eat and where I eat. I have been painfully reminded multiple times that I cannot just take a bite of something as I pass through the kitchen and expect to swallow it without fluids. I cannot be without my water bottle. Ever. I recently left it at home on purpose, however, when I took our dog for a short walk, knowing that there was a foot of new, clean snow on the ground that I could grab every so often to provide moisture to my mouth and throat. Otherwise, it is always nearby. There are days that the unrelenting mouth stuff drives me absolutely insane, but most days I simply try to adjust. There are other days that my neck pain is worse, and I have a heightened awareness of the progressive fibrosis going on in my muscles, especially on the right side that was hit so hard by the damaging radiation beams. I have lost range of motion, for sure, and it feels as if the muscle is shortening and tightening daily. Physical therapy doesn't seem to be helping much at this point, but God continues to use the weaknesses from my cancer to show me things about myself and to display His strength in me.

I am learning the hard way that I have the ability to choose to complain, grumble, or worry, or I can choose to trust. When the answers don't come, or when He doesn't give the answers I am hoping for, I still have to trust Him. That should be easy, after all that He has carried me through and after all that I have learned, and yet it isn't. It is a process. I don't know if cancer will ever come back, which, in a way, forces me to trust. I am still learning that I have to repeatedly lay all of it down at His feet and trust Him, moment by moment. I know in my heart that I can completely trust God for my tomorrows. He is the same yesterday, today, and tomorrow, and He holds my future in His hands. He has seen each of my days already and has a plan for each one. But somehow I still doubt.

Unfortunately, there are no guarantees in this life, but I know that I can trust Him because of who He is and what He has done. Hope. It's all I have.

So what do I do with the doubt? The fear? The anxiety? I choose to trust. I put my trust in the sovereign God of the universe. I know that He is God alone. He is good and He is in control. He has my future in His loving, sovereign, and powerful hands, and I am confident that whatever the future brings, He is with me in it. He has taught me to face adversity and pain with strength, hope, and faith.

CHAPTER 26

Chosen and Changed

The other day, Danica darted through the living room, as she often does, and quickly showed me a short music video she made on the iPad as a tribute to me. She is constantly making music videos right now, but this one was extra special. It was such a gift to me and showed a little bit of her perspective on my cancer race. The first photo is one of her holding a piece of blue construction paper with "She Beat Cancer!" written in big Sharpie letters. The video then moves to a picture of me in the infamous chemo suite wearing red boxing gloves. In that picture, I was standing next to my chemo pump with a sign that said "THE FINAL ROUND." The video continues through several pictures of the two of us together, including some from our recent trip to Lake Tahoe and Yosemite. I marveled at the pictures she happened to choose: chemo pictures, wig pictures, current pictures. The video ends with a selfie of her displaying a big, toothy grin. I could hear the faint sound of upbeat pop music playing in the background. Then I realized it was Meghan Trainor's song, "Mom," and I heard the words "she loves me like nobody else." The title at the bottom of the screen says, "My mom had cancer but she beat it! I admire her so much, she really is the bomb!" What a gift for her to have watched her mama suffer so much and to cherish me and our relationship in that way. Beautiful.

This race was so hard on our children. Each struggled in their own way. At seventeen years of age, and with his tendency to hold things in, Kyle was devastated at first and then slowly pulled away. He was obviously a young man at the time, so some of this was to be expected, but it was painful. Maybe some of it was because the possibility of losing his mom was too difficult to face. Avery has a completely different personality and tends to talk his way through emotional things a bit more. This period of time was no exception. He wore his emotions where we could see them and allowed for some hard discussions here and there. Carter is the one we thought would be a mess when cancer threw off his routine and when things weren't in control. He surprised us, in a way, and handled the change and stress better than we thought. Each of my beautiful children dealt with their emotions differently, but our Danica possibly struggled most of all. At the tender age of seven, she had to grapple with so much. She is the only girl in our house of big, strong, loud boys. She didn't fully understand why her mama disappeared for a couple days each week and why I was sicker every time I walked back in the door. She watched with a completely different set of eyes as my appearance changed and my hair fell out. Thankfully, our girl is a talker, and she is at a pure age when she talks to me about nearly everything. She has asked me some very hard questions and opened up about many of her own fears and emotions. She was terribly afraid of losing her mama and is still afraid of things that can steal life: car accidents, storms. illnesses. She couldn't understand why God allowed her mama to get cancer when she appeared to be so healthy. There is no doubt that this season of her life will help to shape the rest of it, so I guess, in a way, I'm glad she thinks I'm the bomb!

We have tried to teach our children that our loving, mighty, powerful, and sovereign God is where life starts. That He spoke the world into existence and created each of us in His image, exactly to His specifications. That He created each of us for His glory. Me. You. Our God conquered giants, called out kings, shut the mouth of lions, and told the dead to rise. He is the One who rules nations, sustains the universe, calms the seas, and tells the sun when to rise each morning. He certainly does not abandon us and leave us to chance when things get hard.

The God of the universe was not surprised by my cancer diagnosis; in fact, He knew this part of the story before it was written. He numbered my days before I was born and He chose me. He created me perfectly for His glory and provided me with a firm foundation in Him and in my family. He placed me in this great mountain community, surrounded me with people who love me, and even trained me as a speech/language pathologist for a reason. In his perfect sovereignty, He brought Nurse Mark to me twenty-three years ago as a young firefighter and paramedic, giving him a medical background so that he could take perfect care of me later. He gave me each of my beautiful children, each with their unique personality and gifts. Each uniquely designed to love their mama through this in their own way. Powerful.

Long before lumps and biopsies, God, in His unfailing love, was lining up the details for this story. He sent me to Dr. Tritle, He directed me to the Mayo Clinic, He kept me off of the operating table, He put the army together to care for our family, He carefully directed the radiation beams and the chemo poison, He protected my eyes, my ears, my teeth, and my voice, and He provided grace and strength when I didn't have my own.

All that said, I don't have to be afraid that He is going to leave me hanging when life gets scary. Even pain, illness, uncertainty, and suffering are under His control. I remember praying fervently throughout each radiation treatment under that scary mask. Thirty to forty minutes each, five times a week, for seven weeks. That's well over a thousand minutes! It was so obvious that I was not in control, and I was fully aware that there was nothing I could do other than pray and try to trust. I prayed more than I have ever prayed in my life during those helpless moments strapped to a table with my head bolted down. I absolutely couldn't do it on my own. I tried to pray the minutes away by asking God to direct each powerful ray of radiation to exactly where it needed to go. I prayed specifically for protection over my brain, my eyes, my voice, my swallow, and for each tiny little hair cell in my ears. I prayed that He would carefully guide the multiple poisonous, cancer-killing chemotherapy drugs that flowed through my veins throughout my course of treatment. I prayed that the chemo would be used for good, ridding my body of every cancer cell in its path. I prayed that I had more time left to be a wife and a mom. It wasn't always easy to pray, and I struggled at times to trust.

It can be hard to trust God when things are running along smoothly, but it definitely gets harder to trust Him when disaster and pain are knocking the door down. We all want to trust God when things get difficult, and probably every one of you reading this book has struggled with trusting Him on some level or at some point in your life. Even though I am certain that my foundation is rock-solid, and I know He is in control, I still doubt. I still struggle to trust. I still wonder, "When does it become okay to hope again?"; "Is it normal to wonder about tomorrow?"; "How will I respond if my mouth and throat never heal?"; and "What if the cancer comes back?"

I still have a lot of unanswered questions, but He has given me peace. He knows my heart and has heard my prayers, many of which have been answered. I remind all of my precious children that we can trust God simply because of who He is. He is trustworthy and He is our source of hope even when the answers don't exist.

I don't specifically remember asking God why, but I know I was thinking it on some level throughout this race. It is a question that probably every person asks at some point in their life and is often a normal human response when things get hard. The question can be paralyzing and can leave us angry and bitter, but God has never promised that our lives would be free of the hard things. We live in a culture where most people think we get what we deserve. And most people think we all deserve a good, happy life. This simply isn't true. We are all vulnerable to difficulties and pain, but difficulties are not an indication that God doesn't love us or that He is not paying attention. Quite the opposite is actually true. He loves us unconditionally and ultimately knows what is best for each one of us. His purposes are bigger than ours. He knows what is best when a mom in her forties is diagnosed with stage IV cancer and she has four amazing, active kids to finish raising.

Those four active kids have been part of what feels like an ongoing stream of illnesses, injuries, and multiple trips to the emergency room over the last few years. Cancer is behind us for now, but we have had multiple broken bones, septic tank disasters, crippling medical debt, flat tires, car problems, and more than one totaled vehicle. The list goes on and the questions, doubt, and fear can creep back in. Somehow, now when I get the dreaded phone call where someone on the other end of the line says, "Avery was just hit in the face with a baseball and has a broken nose."

or "I think Carter just broke his collar bone," I stay calm. I say, "Okay, I will be right there." There is no more panicking, no freaking out, just a matter-of-fact response of "Let's get this done." God has proven to me that He is in control and has even what seems like an emergency in His loving hands.

It is so easy to forget what I have learned, and I often have to be reminded again and again. I forget the great things that God has done. Although our family has had some gut-wrenching and difficult years, seeming almost impossible at times, we have been stretched and grown through them. I know that tomorrow is still uncertain. It remains an unknown for me and for each one of you holding this book in your hands. Unknown things are scary and can cause fear to well up in me like never before. The doubts and fears of tomorrow still have the potential to cripple me if I let them. But then God, in His perfect timing, reminds me of all He has done and that He is in charge of my tomorrows.

I have definitely learned more of who God really is when I am desperate and things are hard.

Coming to the end of myself changed things, and cancer changed my perspective.

My plans to leave town yesterday by a certain time didn't work out for a number of reasons, and I was completely discouraged. To be honest, I was irritated and impatient. I like to be on time and I like schedules and plans. After my late start, and after braving the icy highway in a crazy January snowstorm for two long hours and passing multiple vehicles and 18-wheelers that had slid off the road, I finally arrived at my hotel around five. I crossed paths with a woman in the hotel lobby as I was checking in. She and her husband were passing through Sedona from Colorado and were on their way to Phoenix. Our casual conversation brought about the subject of my book. She and her husband shared with me the details of a recent accident where she received a head injury and has had a long road of recovery. This was a sweet glimpse of God's perfect timing and sovereignty. We shared some common thoughts and reflections about God's goodness and miraculous care for us as we make our way through difficult circumstances. He obviously planned for me to meet this sweet couple at exactly that moment. Had I been on my seemingly perfect, planned-out schedule, I would have missed seeing God in that moment.

As I sit in front of my computer in Sedona with the intention of bringing this amazing story of God's strength and provision during a season of intense suffering to a close, I have a lot to reflect on. I am blessed. I am in Sedona for three days all by myself to focus on who God is and what He has done. I am charged with the huge task of finishing this story. I am seated on a cute little red couch in my studio hotel room after a morning walk/run (not much running, of course) along a beautiful golf course lined with ponds and streams. The snow-covered red rocks on the horizon are breathtaking. I brought yummy things to eat and snack on this weekend and enjoyed a healthy breakfast of scrambled egg whites with spinach, ham, cheese, and avocadoes. Next to my eggs were several slices of fresh tomatoes and a big slice of cantaloupe. I am delighting in the little things. Did I mention that I am all by myself for three whole days? That is miraculous in and of itself.

As I sip my French press coffee loaded with half and half and a dash of raw sugar and look out my window, I am reminded that His mercies are new every morning and His faithfulness is great. He is the God of the universe who holds all of me in His tender, loving, merciful, and mighty hands. Of course I have plans for my future, but His plans are usually different than mine—and they're usually better.

I am not sure what the future holds, but I know that He is the one who holds it. By His amazing grace, I will continue to run whatever race He has for me by His grace and in His strength. I will run with awareness that my trials in this life are far from over. I know that I will face more challenges, more hurts, and certainly more disappointments, yet, I know that my faith doesn't rest on my circumstances or my healing. Our bodies fail us. People fail us. Life fails us.

God doesn't fail us.

He has already written my story, no matter what tomorrow brings. So I can rest in His strength, His sovereignty, and His unshakable love. I pray that I can get out of the way and that He can use my story, my unfinished and messy story, for His glory.

REFLECTIONS

It has become so clear that I am incapable of completing this race called life on my own. I need Him and I need others. Time and time again, He sent me just the right someone to walk with me through the pain and mess. He sent the runner who came in first in the 10K. I had never even seen him before and still do not know his name. This athletic stranger looked me in the eye, handed his medal to me, and said, "I don't know you, but I came here to run this race for you today." God must have known I needed that, too.

This long, painful race had been clearly marked out for me long before I ever knew I had cancer. In His perfect sovereignty, God had plans to show me just who He is and how much I need Him; not just for challenging races of suffering and difficult things, but in everyday life. This grueling cancer race wasn't really even about me. It was not an individual race, but a huge community effort—one that I would run in His strength and with others running alongside me, picking me up over and over to help me cross a finish line that was never where I thought it would be.

This story is not one of individual achievement or my perseverance, but one of complete and utter reliance on God's perfect provision and my need for help. It certainly wasn't glamorous, or neat, and the finish line seemed to move on me all the time. I now realize there is no finish line—at least not one on this earth. Heaven is my ultimate finish line and my race will continue until then. In the meantime, it is my heart's desire is to reflect Him and give Him the glory, even when life gets hard. I can keep my eyes on the finish line because my trust is in a Savior who sent His only son to take on my sins and die in my place.

If any of you reading my story are thinking I must be a religious person, I want you to understand that this is not about "religion", but rather a personal relationship with my Savior. My faith is in His Son, Jesus. My sin had separated me from a holy God, but He sent His eternal Son to take on sin and to pay the penalty I deserved. God grants forgiveness of sin and gives eternal life to all who trust Him as the One who died in their place. Christ changed my life years ago and my faith in Him is what carried me through every step of this grueling race.

As I bring this story to a close, I am in a different place than when I sat down at the computer for the first time about a year and a half ago. With cancer behind me now by three years, God is still showing me things about Him and about myself. I look back on this race and the symbolism of that race day with humility and awe. When I bump into someone in that purple shirt somewhere, it takes me right back to the dusty trails of Buffalo Park. I see purple and I am instantly reminded that God had every detail of this race planned out before any of us knew I had cancer. This is a truth I need to keep hearing. He is the one who called me to run it, He organized the race and kept moving the finish line, He stripped me of my strength so I would rely on His, and He provided the help I needed to finally step across that line.

P.S. I still hate to run.

Acknowledgments

This is hard. We have been blessed, ministered to, and carried by so many people, and I so badly do not want to forget anyone. Words cannot adequately express our gratitude, and it feels as if these silly words are just not enough. Picture with me, for a moment, this race. Picture countless personalities and gifts showing up, coming alongside our family during every part of it, ministering to us in whatever way God had called them to.

First to my Savior, my strength, and my all in all: The author and finisher of my faith. You gave me life. Thank you for creating me just the way you designed me and for mapping out all of my days before I was born. Thank you for how you put my story together and for trusting me to run this race. Thank you for the scars I bear and for the lingering effects of radiation that keep me in full reliance on You.

To my precious and perfect family: You know me better than anyone else. You know the good, the bad, the hard, and the most painful. Thank you for loving me and for walking this ugly road with me. You have loved me well and have each given me blessings in your specific personality and gifts. Being a wife and a mama to all of you is my favorite thing and is what makes my life full. I couldn't love you more.

To our parents: Alan and Virginia Strnad, and Don and Darlene Wilson. You have loved us and our children as only parents can do. You have fought for us on your knees, and you have lived life in a way that constantly points us to our Savior. You have shown us how to pray and how to trust when life is a mess. Mom and Dad, you have shown me humility and modeled for me how to serve others.

To our brothers, sisters, aunts and uncles, nieces and nephews: God has blessed us with a crazy, amazing, fun, talented family! You have prayed us all the way through this race, and I am honored to call each of you my family. To my one and only brother, Paul, for the hours you spent just sitting with me and being there for me. Time is such a sweet gift. Thank you for giving it freely. To Brenda, for my treasure box of scripture, for organizing house cleaners, for picking up kids, for doing laundry, and for being brave enough to cut off my scraggly pony tail when I asked you.

To Jim and Mary for your faithful support during this trial and for joining forces to pray.

To my girlfriends: Where would I be without you? You have loved me selflessly. You have laughed with me and you have cried with me. To my most precious and bosom friend, Anita: I have known you since our early days in graduate school. We have walked together through both wonderful things and heartbreaking things. We have truly been soul mates and kindred spirits from the day we first met, just like Anne with an *e* and Diana Berry of Green Gables. "True friends are always together in spirit." To my school mamas: Ashley, Holly, Stacy, and Alyssa; and to my sports mamas: Kaye, Michelle, Kelly, Becky, Kathi, Kari, and Veronica— for walking with me through hard things.

To Beth and Rachel for your heroic acts throughout this mess. For your tears and prayers and for the gift of nicknames, music, and cotton candy machines. To Emily, for literally making our house sparkle and for cleaning our gross showers with vinegar. I still can't get them to look like that!

To FCF: Thank you for your faithfulness. You aren't just a cool, stone building downtown where we go on Sunday mornings; you were the hands and feet of Jesus lived out in the form of tears, worship, prayers, cards, fresh-baked cookies on our doorstep, and homemade meals left on our kitchen counter. Thank you for the gift of the iPad that got us through those out of town times and days away from our precious children. Thank you, Pastor Steve, for faithfully praying for me each and every Sunday (and probably all week long) for the better part of two years; I finally had to ask to be taken off the prayer list! To the FCF ladies specifically, for walking with me still and for allowing me to be a part of your lives and ministry.

To the Flagstaff Fire Department, our extended family: A special thank you for joining forces to cover Mark's shifts for the months we were traveling back and forth to Phoenix for my treatment. Your sacrifice allowed me to have him by my side through all of it. And thank you for feeding my family when I couldn't do it. Great emergency response! To Barb Romero for your commitment to fire department families when they are hurting. What a blessing you are to many! Also to Scott McDonald and members from Phoenix Fire Department and other valley departments.

To Northland Rural Therapy and Associates and Kristine Coons for pitching in to cover my precious clients and school contracts and for allowing me to take the time I needed to heal.

To Judy King: What can I say? Words are definitely not enough to express my gratitude for doing months of evaluations for me without getting paid! And thank you for still wearing that purple shirt!

To Steve and Michelle Philpott: Thank you for pizookies, barbeque ribs, and pot roasts! To be able to count on such a wonderful meal for my family each week was amazing. What a blessing you are to us!

To Dave and Kaye Anderson: Thank you for partnering with us in prayer and friendship and for providing housing to us in Scottsdale when we didn't know what to do. Thank you for your visits and for my beloved steak dinner at the Outback when I could finally eat normal food again. We look forward to years of continued friendship and more trips to the Outback!

To all of the amazing, talented, and wise medical professionals who followed their intuition to move quickly and to spend countless hours searching for the point of origin of my cancer: Thank you for your tender care for me during this long journey. Thank you, Nate Tritle, for listening to your gut on that February day in your office and for clearing your busy schedule to do my biopsy that very day. Thank you for your prompt house calls when emergencies arose or when I simply couldn't muster up the strength to be seen in your office. Thank you for your faithfulness and for showing our family that you care. Dr. Michelle Halyard—You are so smart, so thorough, and yet so tender and compassionate when you need to be. Save Avery a seat at the Mayo School of Medicine!

To Dr. Hinni: Thank you for treating Dave Ondrejech so well and for your skill and confidence. I know you would have done exceptional work, but I am quite thankful to have avoided the operating table altogether. Keep up the good work!

To Sheri: The Mayo nutritionist I swore to loathe for all of eternity. I knew right away that we were sisters in Christ, which was another part of God's perfect plan in this mess. Although I really didn't want to like you and all you had to say about the PEG tube and my nutrition disaster, I eventually had to submit myself to your wisdom and care during one of the grossest, most dreaded experiences of my life. Thank you, thank you, thank you! I am alive and well thanks to the combined efforts of you, Nurse Mark, and the infamous "scandi-shake"!

Thank you to all of my talented radiation technicians and to all of my chemo nurses. You were all kind and compassionate and I could feel your care and concern for me all through this battle, and I knew you were rejoicing with me when it was over.

To Michelle and Barbie for doing my hair for free and for being tender to me when my hair was falling out and growing back in crazy. Crying with you during that time, Michelle, was a gift. You made a painful time more bearable.

To Robert and Joanna Ignace, Dave and Kaye Anderson, Barbara Berry, and Brett and Heidi Mierendorf for your graciousness in providing housing for us.

To my friends and family members who were willing to read, re-read, and give me much needed feedback about this story. Thank you, Aunt Linda, for your journalism experience that you pulled from as you edited my story in the very beginning and to Rory Faust, for taking time away from your wife and boys to edit this work. I appreciate your time so much! To my longtime friend, former Pioneer Girls co-leader, and one of Kyle's youth leaders, Kaci Lundgren, for taking this project on as if it were your own and for all of the hours you spent thinking about how to help me develop my ideas, thoughts and emotions even more. Thank you for your gift of passion, commitment and time. Thank you, Casey Ebert, for your thorough, professional help with final editing.

Thank you to all of you who encouraged me, prayed with me, cried with me, faithfully sent me cards (Kathy Robson, Linda Jensen, and Barb Romero), gave us the gift of money, sent us gift cards, gas cards, coffee cards, and Safeway gift cards. Thank you, Cousin Mindee, for my amazing pajamas and to you and Aunt Linda for my Kindle. Thank you Ashley Peak and Gwen Dobbs for your careful thought put into special gifts at just the right time. Thank you to those of you who paid for something without us knowing. We truly would not have made it without you!

Lastly, thank you to all of you who followed my story on CaringBridge and prayed faithfully for me and my family, and to those of you who are hearing this story for the first time. If it is in your hands, I pray that it touches you in some way and shows you a little more of who our God is.

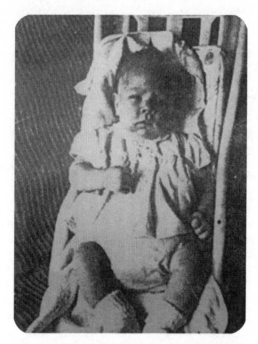

First photo of me from the adoption agency. 1968

Laura and Paul in Alaska, 1972

A proud dad at Laura's high school graduation,
1986 (blue heels not pictured).

Kyle, Avery, Carter and Danica, Fall. 2009

Laura and Mark, New Year's Eve. 2012

The beginning of our journey at the Mayo Clinic
in Scottsdale, Arizona. February 2013.

Avery's baseball team wearing their wristbands for me. February 2013.

The Strnad clan during their Spring Break
visit at the hotel. March 2013.

Kyle's Tucson game during Spring Break. March 2013.

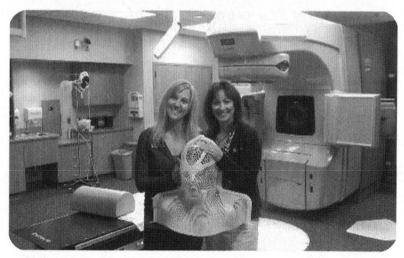

Laura and Anita posing with the "dreaded mask." March 2013.

Mark's parents with us in Phoenix. March 2013.

Week Three with bandaged neck burns. April 2013.

The family on Kyle's senior football night. October 2013.

A special walk with a mouse. November 2013.

Survival calories and new tastes. October 2013.

Adjusting to the wig. November, 2013.

No more wig! April 2014.

Routine nasendoscopy with Dr. Michelle Halyard. August 2014.

Bidding farewell to the mask that saved my life. September 2014.

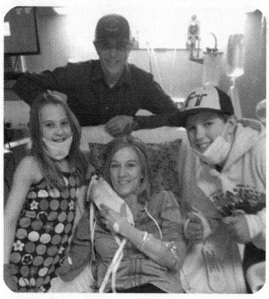

Back in the hospital with cellulitis and strep
in my bloodstream. January 2015.

Celebrating God's goodness with my treasured family as life
begins to look a little more "normal," December 2014.

Made in the USA
Columbia, SC
29 November 2017